WEST COUNTRY MARITIME
AND SOCIAL HISTORY:
SOME ESSAYS

Edited by

Stephen Fisher

University of Exeter

University of Exeter

1980

ISBN   O   85989   121   6

CONTENTS

The Department of Economic History of the University of Exeter is grateful to the Renwick Group for financial support which has made possible the publication of this volume in the customary format of the *Exeter Papers in Economic History*.

INTRODUCTION

With one exception the papers below were presented in recent years at maritime history seminars organised by the Department of Economic History of Exeter University and held at Dartington Hall. The exception is Bruce May's discussion of the rise of Ilfracombe as a seaside resort, which was originally prepared for a Civic Society conference. Its inclusion here complements well the maritime and social issues dealt with in the other contributions, concerned as it is with the functional adaptation of a traditional maritime community.

Again with one exception the papers all relate to the West Country. The odd man out here is Campbell McMurray's consideration of the ship-board status of the early steam engineers, with its national if not international perspective. However, while the other papers may be seen as essays in local history, like all such investigations they have a potentially far broader appeal, given the evidence and insights they can offer on general issues. Good local history provides valuable building blocks for the national and wider historian. Moreover, given the relative paucity of work in recent years on British regional maritime subjects[1] these essays have a particular interest.

All the essays are concerned with the nineteenth century, a time in Britain of much economic and social innovation. The likeness of economy and society to organic life, with the constant waning of some forms and activities and their adaptation and replacement by new growth, is very evident in the pages below. The papers illuminate not only traditional maritime activities but also the effects wrought by new demands and technologies, the general play of market and institutional forces. We can observe the rise and fall of trades and shipping employments, the changing fortunes and functions of havens, the rise of service activities such as nautical education, as well as the reactions of entrepreneurs to new opportunities and of seamen to occupational change.

Thus, David Kennett and Richard Pearse increase our knowledge of the operation of traditional mercantile sailing vessels by their studies of two individual cases, a Cornish-owned 119-ton schooner engaged largely in British trade with the Mediterranean in the 1830s and a Cornish- and Devon-owned 62-ton sloop almost invariably employed in the coastal trades during the fourteen years from her building to her loss in 1866. Voyage itineraries, cargoes, earnings and costs are analysed in detail, using the surviving accounts. Both authors discuss profitability, an important, yet, because of incomplete data, difficult matter, such incompleteness ruling out, for example, any estimates of rates of return on capital invested. Profit calculations are also qualified by the owners' practice in the schooner's case of apparently charging lower than normal freight

---

1 Shipping and shipping services, trade and ports, for example, studied at the local or regional level figure relatively little in recent bibliographies of published work in the *Economic History Review*.

rates on their own consignments – if at all widespread this practice has serious implications for the attempts by historians to assess shipping profitability. While the schooner made good returns in terms of income over operating costs, the sloop did much less well, reflecting perhaps a higher degree of competition in the coastal shipping business and the impact on such business of the spreading railway system. In analysing voyage earnings Pearse shows how, from 1859, in the second half of the sloop's career, overall voyage times lengthened while neither the rate of earnings nor of disbursements increased, which much reduced the net returns – a nice demonstration of the importance of quick sailing and fast turn-rounds in ports for shipping profits. This vessel's low net earnings remind one of Craig's observation that ownership of small vessels in this period could be regarded as a kind of 'subsistence economy', with low returns for shareholders but a gratifying award of independence and status to owners and masters.[1] Putting notions of profit on one side Kennett aptly points to the social good a ship could do, through the employment created in its building, fitting-out and maintenance as well as its actual sailing.

In contrast to these enquiries into traditional maritime economy, John Lucking's paper, while dealing with a well-established activity, the Post Office packet service, focuses on innovation with first the starting in 1794 of a regular Channel Isles service from Weymouth, followed by further innovation in 1827, with the replacement of the sail vessels by steam-driven packets. Eighteen years later the Weymouth service was brought to an end by another innovation in steam, the coming of the London & South Western Railway to Southampton, and the slight but significant shortening of journey time this gave that port in the crucial London – Channel Isles mail and passenger traffic over the more westerly Weymouth. Although a Weymouth packet service was never revived, a commercial steam service to the islands was opened in 1857, when with Weymouth's accession to the railway system the port again became competitive. Lucking's paper thus illustrates the changes on the seas wrought by the coming of steam in the guise of both steamship and rail-way. It further contains much information on the conduct of the cross-Channel services, the actual vessels employed, and the turn from privately-owned sailing packets to government ownership of the steam vessels (because of the private shipowners' uncertainty over the expense of a steam service). Consideration is given also to the employment and other benefits brought by the packets. Lucking's paper, it will be apparent, has a wide interest, and may be seen as not only contributing to the history of the Post Office and Weymouth but as illuminating the rise of Channel Isles tourism.

Campbell McMurray's paper also revolves around steam at sea. This investigation has a pioneering quality in that it attempts to assess the social status of marine engineers in the early decades of steam navigation.

---

1   Robert S Craig, 'Shipowning in the south-west in its national context, 1800-1914', in Stephen Fisher and Walter Minchinton, eds. *Transport and shipowning in the west country* (University of Exeter, 1973) pp.36-8.

This is done by considering, at least in the case of the larger vessels, how engineers were recruited, their reception on board, and their own perception of their position. In approaching these problems thoughtful use is made of the social psychologist's concept of 'relative deprivation'. A plausible case is argued that the feelings of deprivation and grievance apparent among ships' engineers in the later nineteenth century were not likely to have been generally felt by the first practitioners. McMurray considers marine engineers may well have retained as their principal normative reference group the shore-based engineers, themselves part of the skilled artisan class and 'labour aristocracy' of the age. Their position on board was 'relatively privileged', being roughly congruent with that of the tradesmen, while they were better paid than even the mates, coming second, although distinctly so, only to the masters. Such a position was not likely on the whole to have generated unfavourable status comparisons with others on board. An appendix to the paper presents passages from a conversation McMurray once had with a retired ship's engineer who was at sea in the early years of the present century. It demonstrates well how the historian can gain both evidence and insight from oral reminiscence.

McMurray has something in common with another of our authors, Alston Kennerley, in that both men were drawn to their subjects by professional mercantile sea experience, McMurray being himself a former ship's engineer and Kennerley a deck officer with a master's certificate. McMurray is now with the National Maritime Museum, while Kennerley lectures in the Faculty of Maritime Studies at Plymouth Polytechnic. This Faculty is in fact a direct successor to one of the two Plymouth educational institutions Kennerley considers in his paper, the School of Navigation. Set up in 1862 by local interests and with financial and other support from the national Department of Science and Art, it was followed in 1877 by the Training Ship *Mount Edgcumbe*. This establishment, accommodated in a converted fifty-five year old man-of-war moored on the river Tamar, and intended for the instruction of boys in the craft of seamanship, was also the product of local initiatives with governmental, including Admiralty, support. Both institutions owed much to the rising mid-nineteenth century interest, local and national, in education, and to a special concern with the standards of mercantile officers and the supply of seamen. Kennerley's paper thus bears on the history of British technical education, a subject of interest given that tardy and inadequate development in this field is thought by some to have been significant in Britain's relatively declining economic performance in the decades prior to 1914.[1] Both institutions clearly helped to raise the competence of seafarers, although by the end of the nineteenth century it seems they were becoming less appropriate to the times. The training ship found its ideals frustrated by the ending of the seaman apprenticeship system and the unwillingness of many steam shipping owners to employ boys. Opinion too was moving against the use of ships as training establishments on grounds of health

1   See, for example, Derek H Aldcroft and Harry W Richardson, *The British economy 1870-1939* (Macmillan, 1969) esp. pp.147-51.

and safety. In the end the *Mount Edgcumbe* failed to make the transition
to a land establishment, closing down in 1920. The navigation school
for long had a restricted outlook, throughout its independent life
apparently doing little more than prepare candidates for the masters and
mates examinations. In 1932, after its absorption into the Plymouth and
Devonport Technical College, an especially lean time ensued. From 1949,
however, broadly-based nautical courses began to be developed in Plymouth,
at long last fulfilling the aspirations of some of the original supporters
of the School. Apart from its general interest, Kennerley's paper is
particularly informative on the operation of the training ship. It is
again notable here how oral reminiscence, in this case gleaned from those
who knew the ship in its last years, has proved a valuable source.

Themes of growth and decline and adaptation figure strongly in our
last two papers. Amber Patrick deals with the rise and fall in the
nineteenth century of the inland port of Morwellham, some eighteen miles
up the Tamar from Plymouth. Her focus is on the 1850s and 1860s, when
the quays became a hive of activity with the great local copper mining
bonanza to which Devon Great Consols largely contributed. The rather
scanty documentary evidence that survives is used to discuss the kinds
of trade carried on, mostly copper ore out and coal and limestone in,
and the shipping employed, Tamar barges and coastal trade vessels. Miss
Patrick's estimate that in the peak years of activity some 500 vessels
annually called at Morwellham indicates the importance of her subject.
In an appendix details are presented of a number of the actual vessels
involved in these trades, including their size, place of build and ownership.

Morwellham declined with the decline of Devon Great Consols, the
closure of the mine in 1901 bringing an end to trading at the port. With
the difficulty in devising alternative activities, or in any case the
failure to do so, the busy days of the quays became but a memory.[1] In
contrast, Bruce May's essay on Ilfracombe deals with virtually one long
success story, the seizing by a traditional haven of lucrative new
opportunities. At the close of the eighteenth century Ilfracombe's
fortunes were bound up with coastal trade and fishing, it being as yet
only a tiny watering place. But the burgeoning in England of a class of
leisured well-to-do people turning more and more to active recreation in
the form of seabathing and scenery, gave Ilfracombe its historic chance.
The beauty of the local coastline and countryside, the improving
communications with the coming of the Bristol Channel steam packets in
the 1820s, and not least the response of local entrepreneurs, did the
rest. May analyses many aspects of the town's rise as a select resort,
its population growth and changing occupational structure, the speculative building of more and more streets of residences and lodging
houses, the urban improvements. Along with the steam packet the railway did its bit, its arrival, first in nearby Barnstaple in 1854 and

1   Curiously the last few years have seen a revival of Morwellham's
     former busyness, not as a port but as a maritime and industrial
     museum, its quays in the summer at least thronged with school-
     children and tourists.

then twenty years later in Ilfracombe itself, inducing further growth and a social broadening of the resort's clientele. The town though continued to attract the genteel and the rich, the lavish Ilfracombe Hotel of 1867 including American millionaires and scions of European royal families amongst its guests. With the resort's widening clientele came a growing provision of entertainments, which even as they became more popular in appeal still retained a fitting propriety. May closes his study at the peak of Ilfracombe's prosperity, in 1914. Despite an initial return to old ways, the resort, like so much else in British life, failed to make a full transition to the post-war world, with its new leisure demands. Even today Ilfracombe, at least in its centre, remains much as it was in its heyday, a remarkable legacy of Regency and Victorian taste. May's paper documents well how North Devon produced a seaside resort in the nineteenth century comparable to the more numerous rising South Devon resorts such as Torquay, Dawlish and Teignmouth. It adds to the growing literature on the rise of the leisure and holiday business in Britain, being of special value because of its concern with the more 'up-market' end of that business.

In introducing an earlier set of Exeter maritime history papers, the present editor observed[1] that before a general well-based maritime history of the South West could be written more specialised studies were needed on a variety of subjects - individual ports and their trades, local merchant and shipowning communities, the fishing industry, among others. In his view the present papers distinctly advance our under-standing in a number of important areas, and not only in a regional context. It is notable that all the contributions centre on the nineteenth century. However, that century was one of marked transition in maritime and social affairs in the West Country, and therefore of special interest. It is to be hoped that investigations such as those presented here will stimulate others to enquire into these diverse and intriguing areas of experience, and over broader periods of time. In such promotion and publication of research the Dartington economic history seminars obtain their justification.

March 1980   Stephen Fisher

1   *Ports and shipping in the south-west* (University of Exeter, 1970) pp.ix-x.

ACKNOWLEDGEMENTS

Thanks are due to the Warden of the Devon Centre of Dartington Hall for allowing the maritime history seminar to use such a congenial setting for its discussions. The editor of these papers would also like to thank Celia Manning and Jean Baker for their skilful typing of the manuscripts and William Wood and the staff of the University Printing Unit for their customary efficiency.

THE SOUTH WEST'S OTHER PACKET STATION: WEYMOUTH, 1794 - 1845

John Lucking

Mention Post Office packets and almost certainly one thinks of Falmouth, especially if one's concern is with the South West. The subject of this paper is what may be called the South West's other packet station.

As well as the Falmouth services the Post Office was responsible for a number of short-sea packet routes. These domestic routes, as they were called, no doubt lacked the fame and glamour of the ocean-going services but they were none the less important. Some of them, in fact, were of earlier date than Falmouth, for which they served as a model; and, albeit under different management, and with a little variation here and there, they are still in business, whereas the Falmouth packets have, so to speak, become but a part of our maritime past.

The oldest and most important of the domestic services were those between Harwich and Helvoetsluys, between Dover and Ostend and Calais, and between Holyhead and Dublin, all dating from the seventeenth century or earlier. A northern route to Ireland, by way of Portpatrick and Donaghadee, was opened in 1710, and a southern, by way of Milford and Dunmore, in 1787. To this group of five, in 1794, was added a sixth, serving the Channel Islands and based on Weymouth.

The Channel Islands, loyal to the British Crown but culturally and commercially, as well as geographically, closer to France, had hitherto been largely disregarded from the point of view of postal communication. Between 1778 and 1783, as a result of France's entry into the American War of Independence, a Post Office packet from Dover, the *Express,* Captain Sampson, had maintained a more or less regular service to and from Southampton, but that was an exception. Normally the posts were haphazard. Letters were sent by ordinary trading vessels, mainly through Southampton, but alternatively through Weymouth, Lyme Regis, Brixham, Dartmouth or even Plymouth, as might be convenient.

The island communities appear to have been resigned to that situation, and since a regular packet service was most unlikely to pay its way the Post Office was reluctant to get involved.[1] There was, however, an increasing demand for such a service from the local governors, because of the islands' strategic importance in time of war with France, and the claims of two or three south coast ports, to be considered as the English station in the event of packets being established, were advanced by various interested parties.

1   A count of letters passing to the islands through Southampton in December 1791 gave a figure of 2296, under 30,000 for the year.

Effectively there were two alternatives: to send the mails twice a week by ordinary vessels on freight, at an estimated £300-400 a year, or to send them by an officially appointed packet once a fortnight. Since virtually all Channel Islands freight passed through Southampton the first alternative would have meant the appointment of that port as the packet station; and since the majority of passengers also went that way even an official packet would have cost less than at Weymouth. Nevertheless it was Weymouth that was favoured.

Probably, as the port nearest to the islands, it would have been favoured anyway, since the Post Office made it a rule to prefer the shortest routes by sea, but what seems to have clinched the matter was the town's popularity with George III.[1] Among the king's visitors to Weymouth was the Earl of Chesterfield, joint Postmaster General,[2] whose opinion was that 'if the object in the establishment of Packets to Jersey and Guernsey is expedition and almost a certainty of their sailing whenever the Mail for those Islands arrives, there can be no better and no safer place than the Portland Road ... and there is no wind with which the Packet cannot sail or make a passage'.[3]

The Post Office remained opposed to the whole idea but at the beginning of 1794, after prolonged uncertainty, the government ordered the establishment of Channel Islands packets as a 'matter of state' - or, as we might say today, 'in the national interest' - and appointed Weymouth as the port of departure.

To open the new service two packets were transferred from Dover, where suspension of the Calais service because of war with France had left them for the time being surplus to requirements. These were the *Royal Charlotte* and the *Rover*. It was the *Royal Charlotte* which, on 13 February 1794, had the distinction of making the first crossing. Sailings then continued weekly, on Thursdays - later altered to Saturdays - and by an act of 28 March 1794[4] the arrangements were placed on a proper legal footing.

The packets, although usually designated 'H.M.', were not government-owned but, like those on the other stations, were subject to agreement between the Postmaster-General and the captain, who undertook to provide a suitable vessel, specially built for the service, against a fixed annual payment. This payment, which varied from station to station, was intended to cover running expenses and all risks except that of capture by the enemy in wartime, for which the captain was indemnified by the Revenue at a valuation previously lodged. In practice it did not do so and the difference was made good by the profits from fare-paying passengers. The packets did not carry freight.

---

1   The king and royal family were regular visitors from 1789 to 1805.

2   From 1691 to 1823 the appointment was a dual one.

3   John P Alexandre, 'Early postal service to the Channel Islands', *Bulletin of La Société Jersiaise*, XII (1933) 283.

4   34 Geo III c.18.

The fixed payment at Weymouth was, initially, £795.11.0. The fare between Weymouth and either Guernsey or Jersey was fixed at £1.6.0, of which half a guinea went to the Revenue and the balance to the captain. It is interesting to notice in passing that this was, and remains, the only cross-channel service involving a double port of call, and that the principle of a single uniform fare has applied ever since. Between the islands the captains charged 5/- (focsle 2/6).

The average passage time seems to have been about twenty-four hours between Weymouth and Guernsey and a further eight or ten between there and Jersey, but it could be much longer. Graphic accounts of particularly bad crossings, sent by the captains to the Post Office to explain why the mails were late, make entertaining reading. Incoming mails were sometimes landed elsewhere than at Weymouth - there are records of out-of-course landings at both Swanage and Brixham - and if neither packet was in port when the outward mail arrived recourse was sometimes had to any vessel that happened to be handy. The round trip was spread over about a week.

In addition to the more obvious uncertainties of wind and weather the Channel Islands packets had to contend with other delays and interruptions, which caused the Post Office a good deal of trouble. A peculiarity in the early years was the right of the island governors to delay sailing for any reason they might judge sufficient. This privilege was regularly abused by one Major-General John Small, of Guernsey, whose arbitrary interference often threw the sailing programme into complete disorder, to the annoyance of Post Office and public alike. Quite often, it seems, the packet did not get to Jersey at all, and the mail for that island had to be sent forward from Guernsey as opportunity offered. Passengers and letters from Jersey reverted to ordinary trading vessels sailing to Southampton and, as the Jersey postmaster put it, in reporting to London, the captains 'murmured sadly' at the loss of business.[1] Small was reprimanded by the Home Secretary but to little effect, and the Post Office had to make the best of it until 1796, when he died. The following year the Jersey Lt. Governor applied to have the Guernsey call still further limited, and after discussion at the Post Office it was agreed that in future it need be no more than 'a reasonable time to receive the mails and passengers' instead of the twenty-four hours previously stipulated.[2]

A more persistent problem was smuggling, extensively indulged in the Channel Islands trade, the Guernsey trade in particular.[3] In June 1799, for instance, the *Rover* was seized by the Excise after the discovery of 66 lbs of tobacco and other contraband on board. The following month the packet *Earl of Chesterfield* was also seized.

1   Post Office Records, London (cited hereafter as PO) E685K/1814 XXIV, 4 February 1795.

2   PO E685K/1814, XXXV.

3   The Smuggling Act of 1807 (47 Geo III c.66) made specific reference to 'frauds ... by ships trading from the Islands of Jersey, Guernsey, Alderney and Sark', and U.K. customs officers, whose main concern for many years was surveillance of shipping movements, were still stationed in Jersey and Guernsey until as recently as 1972.

Petitioning the Commissioners of Excise with some eloquence for the
restoration of their vessels both captains contended that however hard
they tried they could not stop it. Francis Freeling, Post Office
secretary, forwarding the petitions through the Postmaster General,
drew attention to what he called the 'unpleasant circumstances',
remarking that the seizures appeared to be 'perfectly justified'. He
commented further that that being so 'any strong Interference with the
Board of Excise by your Lordships cannot with propriety be given ... I
have all Reason to believe [the commanders] were totally ignorant.[1]
Having considered the matter for some weeks the Excise office replied
that as the quantity seized in the *Rover* was 'not very considerable'
that packet would be delivered up on payment of the 'Expences', but the
articles found in the *Earl of Chesterfield* having been 'artfully
concealed, and a great part of them in places contrived for the very
purpose in the Captain's own Cabin' they were of opinion the vessel
should not be restored. 'I am directed to add', the letter went on,
'that it has been suggested ... that the Country is constantly supplied
with some of the Articles in a contraband way by means of the Packets;
that the Seamen declare they could not maintain their Families without
Smuggling; and that the Captains permit each to bring on board much
greater quantities of Spirits and Tobacco than are actually necessary
every Voyage, a Practice so exceedingly pernicious to the Revenue and
the fair Trader that the Commissioners think themselves bound to state
these matters [for] immediate Consideration'[2] - a wry commentary on
the conduct of a government service, and on Freeling's confidence in the
captains' innocence. Eventually the *Earl of Chesterfield* was released,
probably on payment of a substantial fine.

While the Jersiais resented the packets' detention in Guernsey the
Guernesiais had their own grievance. At St Helier the packet entered
the harbour but at St Peter Port it merely lay off, while the mails and
passengers were rowed ashore. This prompted the appearance of unofficial
packets, or bye-boats, serving Guernsey only. From March 1800 the
Enterprize cutter, 'new packet or bye-boat ... seventy tons burthen, well
manned and armed', was advertised from Weymouth and back weekly.[3] The
name of the commander, Amos Le Cocq, suggests that this vessel may have
been Guernsey-based, Le Cocq being a Guernsey name.

The *Enterprize* seems not to have lasted very long, but later a
Weymouth shipowner and shipping agent, Nicholas Robilliard, a native of
Alderney, put on the *Alert* 'Guernsey Extra Packet or Bye-boat;[4] which
by coming alongside in that island proved more convenient to Guernsey
passengers than the official packet. In 1806 John Burnett Bennett,

1   PO E685K/1814, XXXVIII, 22 July 1799.

2   PO E685K/1814, XXXVIII, 5 September 1799.

3   *Sherborne & Yeovil Mercury*, 24 March 1800 *et seq*.

4   *Salisbury & Winchester Journal*, 3 November 1806.

inspector of packets, wrote to Freeling: 'When I was at Weymouth last month I was informed a Bye Boat had been established ... carrying Passengers on those days when the Packet does not Sail, whereby the amount received for Passengers by this office has fallen off from £700 to £400 per annum'.[1] Robilliard also handled many Guernsey letters which, addressed 'care Mr. Nicholas Robilliard, Weymouth', by-passed the official packet, with further loss of revenue.[2]

From time to time it was suggested in the islands that the bye-boat might be taken over as an additional official packet. Hitherto those suggestions had always been turned down on the grounds that as the service had originally been agreed only for the duration of the war it might with the return of peace be discontinued. The fact was that within a year or two it had become part and parcel of island life. Faced with Bennett's report Freeling conceded that the circumstances were now very different, and that there was no intention of the service being withdrawn. Instead, he recommended to the Postmaster General that a third packet, enabling sailings to be increased to twice weekly, should be tried for a year. This started in October 1806 and at the end of the trial period had produced revenue of £1260 for the outlay of £795. Thereafter three packets were Weymouth's regular establishment, and the *Alert* went out of business. Sailings were now on Wednesdays as well as Saturdays.[3]

Thanks partly to their defensive armament, partly to the navy and partly, no doubt, to good luck, the Weymouth packets enjoyed a long immunity from attack. But there is always a first time and on 29 October 1811 the *Chesterfield* was taken prize by a Cherbourg privateer, *L'Epervier*.[4] In accordance with his agreement the Chesterfield's owner and master, Starr Wood, was compensated for the loss, to the value of £1626.7.5.[5] A replacement was laid down and in the meantime Wood had a temporary command, the *Rapid*. For a year all was well. Then one day in October 1812, when the new packet was nearly complete and due for official inspection, Wood and four of his men went to the yard to see to certain last-minute details. They were still away when the *Rapid* was due to sail, so she sailed without them, manned by half a crew in charge of the mate. Even that might have passed unnoticed if the mate had been sober.

1   PO E685K/1814, XLIV, 8 July 1806.

2   J M Y Trotter, 'Guernsey, the franking system & Mr Robilliard', *Bulletin of the Postal History Society*, 122 (1962).

3   PO Post 1/22 (Treasury Letter Books XII) 185, letter from P.M.G. to Treasury, 30 November 1807.

4   Sparrowhawk.

5   PO Post 1/24 (Treasury Letter Books XIV) 226.

In the event the passage appears to have come close to disaster, avoided only because there happened to be two master mariners on board as passengers. Following formal complaint by the Lt. Governor of Guernsey, Wood, the mate and the agent, were all dismissed; but the Post Office had still to hear the last of Wood. His appeal against dismissal having failed he set up in opposition, flying a flag that was a good enough imitation of the real thing to mislead some passengers into thinking that they were boarding the packet.[1] In 1814 Wood transferred what the Post Office called his 'very injurious' opposition to Southampton, but its influence was still felt as he charged only £1 for a passage to the islands instead of the official fare of 26/-. Faced with this undercutting the packet captains felt obliged to do the same, which meant in turn that to maintain their incomes they had to 'adjust' their passenger returns. Actually there was nothing new in that, it was merely a question of degree, but the Post Office countered by varying the terms of the agreements. From then on the hire charge was reduced but the captains kept the whole of the passenger receipts.[2]

In March 1816 the English Channel was crossed for the first time by a steam vessel,[3] and within three or four years commercial steamers operating on both the Dover and Holyhead routes were making serious inroads into the packets' passenger figures. This competition created a dilemma. The packet captains complained bitterly at the loss of income, and demanded compensation, but the Post Office was not convinced that for so important a service as the royal mail steam was really reliable. It was only a matter of time, of course, before its advantages had to be admitted and in the summer of 1821 steam packets took over from sail on both the Dover and Holyhead stations.

Two years later a steamer appeared in the Channel Islands. In June 1823 the *Medina*, built to run between Southampton and the Isle of Wight, was chartered privately for a journey to Guernsey. While there she ran an excursion to Jersey and back and in both islands aroused widespread interest. This prompted Sir Colin Halkett, Lt. Governor of Jersey, to write to the Post Office urging the use of steam for the island mails, preferably via Portsmouth or Southampton.[4] In June 1824 the proprietors

1   PO Post 1/25 (Treasury Letter Books XV) 168-9.

2   PO Post 41/3 (Packet Reports) 353. The average annual loss having been estimated at £300 the hire charge, then standing at £408.16.1, was reduced by £308.16.1 'leaving the commander with £100 plus the passage money'. In 1830, however, the Commissioners of Revenue Inquiry referred to the hire charge as having been reduced to £408.16.1 in 1814 and 'the official proportion of the freight' as having been 'abandoned to the commanders' in 1819. *British Parliamentary Papers (BPP)*, 1830, XIV, Append. 1, 1.

3   The *Margery*. See, H Philip Spratt, *The birth of the steamboat* (Griffin, 1958) p.94.

4   *BPP*, 1830, XIV, Twenty-second Report of the Commissioners of Revenue Inquiry. Part V - Packet Establishment, Append. 19, 3.

of a Portsmouth steamer[1] offered their services. The Bailiff and Royal Court of Guernsey, on the other hand, pleaded that Weymouth 'should not be deserted'; the Post Office, too, preferred Weymouth, and made it clear that if and when steam was introduced that would be the chosen station, and with official packets. The captains knew Weymouth and the shorter crossing could be entrusted to smaller vessels, which were cheaper.[2]

Treasury approval for the establishment of steam packets was given in December 1824, but two and a half years elapsed before steam actually took over. In the meantime the twice-weekly sailings remained in the hands of the cutters *Francis Freeling, Hinchinbrook* and *Countess of Liverpool,* giving rise to an exactly similar situation to that seen at Holyhead and Dover - and reopening in the process the old argument of Weymouth vis-à-vis Southampton. Commercial steamers sailing from the latter port took an increasing proportion of Channel Islands passengers, producing at Weymouth the familiar complaints and claims for compensation.

The situation was not made any easier by the loss of two packets, within the space of a few months. On 2 February 1826 the *Hinchinbrook,* while hove-to off the south-east corner of Alderney to shorten sail, drifted with the current - afterwards estimated at about 7 knots - and went aground.[3] There was no loss of life, the crew and fifteen passengers getting ashore in the ship's boat, but the second loss was a disaster. On the night of 6 September 1826 the *Francis Freeling* set sail from Weymouth and disappeared. Exactly what happened was never established but it was assumed that she had been run down by some unidentified vessel.[4] There were no survivors. It was said that something like a hundred children were left fatherless.

With steam in the offing neither vessel was replaced, the *Countess of Liverpool* being joined by a succession of temporary packets.[5] The change took place eventually on 5 July 1827 and the first mail crossing by steam took place two days later - of which more in due course. To complete the account of sail it still remains to say something about the vessels themselves and their ownership.

1   The *Lord Beresford. BPP,* 1830, XIV, Part V - Packet Establishment, Append, 19, 1.

2   *BPP,* 1830, XIV, Part V - Packet Establishment, Append. 19, 2.

3   *Dorset County Chronicle,* 6 February 1826.

4   *Dorset County Chronicle,* 21 September 1826. A Swedish brig later reported that off Portland Bill she had run down a vessel answering the *Francis Freeling's* description, which she had sighted too late to avoid.

5   The *Dove, Iris* and *Queen Charlotte.*

Excluding miscellaneous vessels pressed into service to meet some emergency the Weymouth sailing packets appear altogether to have totalled fourteen, of which eight may be found in the Weymouth custom house registers. One more appears in the register for the old port of Sandwich. [1] The registers do not, of course, indicate that a vessel was employed as a packet but that information may be gathered from the Post Office archives and the local press. When the name in the register is not in itself a positive identification with the packet service, dates and owners' and masters' names provide a connecting link.

Of the ports whose registrations began with the 1786 Act comparatively few still have their 1786 registers, and of the former packet stations Weymouth is the only one. A rarer survival is that of two volumes of parchment certificate counterfoils, covering all Weymouth registrations from 1801 to 1816.[2] These give certain details not transcribed into the register, such as whether a vessel was measured afloat or aground and, of greater interest, perhaps, in respect of first registrations at least, the name of the builder. Some first certificates also include the date of launch. Counterfoils exist for six of the eight Weymouth-registered packets and it seems reasonable to conclude that despite certain gaps we have a more detailed record for Weymouth than for any other packet station.

The usual type of packet on the domestic routes at this period was a cutter. Apparently no other rig was used - certainly all the Weymouth packets whose rig is recorded were of that type. The type of build is not always recorded but broadly speaking the earlier ones were clinker-built and the later were carvel. The regulation minimum tonnage for a Channel Islands packet was 50, but those recorded ranged from 63 to 107. In length the packets ranged from 53 to 63ft, with a beam of 18 to 20ft or thereabouts (see Appendix 1). The crew numbered up to twenty.[3] In nearly every case the packets were in single ownership, from which it may be inferred that the owners were men of some means; and since replacements were invariably a little bigger than those they replaced it

1   Now preserved in Ramsgate custom house.

2   Preserved, with the Weymouth registers, in Weymouth custom house.

3   When the service was under consideration it was stated PO Post 42/46, Freeling's Minutes, XII, 83, 21 January 1794, that 'Captain Bennet requires 20 men to Wood's 16', and later, when the 1807 Smuggling Act stipulated maximum complements, 'vessels in the service of Government' were exempt. The permitted crew for an ordinary vessel of comparable size was between 6 and 8, according to actual tonnage. In 1830, *BPP*, 1830, XIV, Commissioners of Revenue Inquiry, Part V - Packet Establishment, Appendix, the *Hinchinbrook, Francis Freeling* and *Countess of Liverpool* were quoted as having had a crew of only 9 (commander, master and 7 seamen). The larger crews were no doubt justified by the need to defend the vessel in the event of attack, and it may be assumed that the smaller were the normal peacetime complement.

may also be inferred that the service was found reasonably remunerative - with or without smuggling.[1] The owner was usually also the master, though on that point the register and the Post Office archives are sometimes at variance.

The commanders of the two packets sent originally from Dover, the *Rover* and the *Royal Charlotte,* were respectively Joseph Bennett and James Wood. Bennett was a local man, whose name appears in the Weymouth register as owner or master of other vessels before 1794, including a 114-ton brigantine, the *Peggy.* Wood, on the other hand, transferred with his vessel, on being specially recommended for the appointment by General Conway, Lt. Governor of Jersey. Having served as mate to Captain Sampson in the *Express* he had a good knowledge of Channel Islands waters. In 1795 he took delivery of a newly-built packet, the *Earl of Chesterfield* - the one seized for smuggling - and the *Royal Charlotte* then presumably returned to Dover. At all events nothing more is recorded of her at Weymouth. The register names Wood as owner of the *Earl of Chesterfield* but the master as Starr Wood; Starr was James' son. In the Post Office records, however, James continues to be referred to as master until May 1803, when there is a specific reference to his resignation and to Starr succeeding him. It comes as some surprise that so unimportant a matter as the appointment of a packet captain should have concerned the king, but in the case of Starr Wood that was the case. George III himself was asked to approve the appointment, and we are told that he 'appeared quite pleased that the question had been referred to him by Lord Auckland and Lord Charles Spencer,[2] particularly as it regarded Weymouth'.[3] How homely! but how ironical that it was Starr Wood who was later involved in the affair of the *Rapid* (cited above) and fell so badly from grace! The *Earl of Chesterfield* was taken off the mail run in November 1806 and the following month was advertised for sale by auction (see Appendix 3). No change of ownership is recorded in the register, however; the vessel is merely shown as broken up in 1811. Her replacement (whose capture by the French privateer in 1811 was the beginning of all Wood's troubles) was the *Chesterfield.*[4]

The additional packet of 1806 was the Guernsey-registered *General Doyle,* Captain Charles Pipon. The *General Doyle* first appears in the Weymouth register in June 1807, Pipon being shown as owner with Isaac Malzard as master, but the only master mentioned in the Post Office records is Pipon. When the permanent establishment was made up to three

1   Since they depended on passengers it was, of course, in their interest to provide as good a vessel as possible.

2   Joint Postmasters General.

3   PO Post 35/4 (P.M.G's Minutes) 228.

4   Wood's new packet of 1812, built to replace the captured one, was also called *Chesterfield;* the two should not be confused with one another, or with the *Earl of Chesterfield* (see Appendix 1).

Pipon became both owner and master of the *Francis Freeling*, and the *General Doyle* returned to Guernsey. In 1814 the *Francis Freeling* was sold to Frederick White, another name already in the register as owner or master and one destined to be long associated with the packets.

The *Rover* remained on the run for nearly twenty years - longer than any of the others. When her registry was transferred to Weymouth, in December 1799, Bennett was shown as owner and Thomas Quirk as master but here again, for what significance it may have, the records are at variance. Quirk, who had sailed with Bennett as mate in the *Peggy*, did the same in the *Rover*, and sometimes took command, but he does not appear in the Post Office packet books as master until July 1804, when Bennett retired. On being withdrawn from service, in 1813, the *Rover* was broken up. Her replacement was the *Hinchinbrook*, of which Quirk retained ownership until she was lost. For a few months he then commanded the *Queen Charlotte* and was then retired on pension.

The vacancy caused by Starr Wood's dismissal was filled by Robert Naylor, lately in command of a Falmouth packet. For the Channel Islands service he built the *Countess of Liverpool*, launched in November 1813 and registered the following February with Naylor as both owner and master. Only two days after the vessel was registered, however, he was obliged by debt to dispose of a one-eighth share, and within another month of two further eighths. He retained command and a five-eighths share until May 1816, when his debts finally overwhelmed him and his remaining share passed to his creditors. He then resigned.[1] For a time the *Countess of Liverpool* was replaced by the Ramsgate cutter *Sir William Curtis*, resuming service in June 1817 when the Post Office appointed Robert White in Naylor's place. Two months later White acquired the five-eighths share held by Naylor's creditors, and in due course a further one-eighth, but he never became sole owner and the *Countess of Liverpool* is a notable exception to the usual pattern of ownership. In 1825 command was transferred to Richard White.

In May 1826, in anticipation of the arrival of steam packets, the Post Office appointed Richard Wilkinson, lately in command of the *Greyhound*, revenue cruiser, as an additional master. Four months later he went down in the *Francis Freeling*, while relieving Frederick White, and Ross Connor, Lt. R.N., was appointed in his place. Like Bennett, Quirk and the Whites, both Wilkinson and Connor were local men. It is interesting, too, to notice a marked family element among these local commanders. The Whites were all related, James and Starr Wood were father and son, as already mentioned, Quirk was Bennett's son-in-law and Connor was related to the Whites.

II

With the change to steam the Post Office packet service was placed on a different footing, the steam packets being government-owned instead of hired from private owners. When steam was about to be introduced at Dover

1   PO Post 41/2 (Packet Reports) 488.

the captains there were given the opportunity of continuing the existing arrangement but 'steam being in its infancy', as they put it, and they 'not having had any experience to enable them to form an estimate of the expense of navigating and maintaining steamers'[1] they declined. I am not aware that a similar offer was made elsewhere but no doubt if it had been the answer would have been the same. In any case the very much heavier outlay involved with steam vessels made some sort of corporate ownership more appropriate.

The virtue of hiring was that it offered close control without full responsibility. If the captains were neither able nor willing to continue that arrangement there were two alternatives, commercial contract or Crown ownership. The former was mistrusted as unreliable; the latter had long been objected to as uneconomic and inefficient, but was nevertheless the course adopted. Against its own better judgment the Post Office thus turned shipowner, and between 1821 and 1826 became responsible for a considerable fleet of steam vessels - a specialised job for which it was not qualified and which it undertook without enthusiasm. One by one, with the exception of Harwich,[2] the domestic stations turned over to steam. Weymouth was the last.

Continuity of management between old and new was ensured by retention of the agent, and many of the other personnel were also retained, including Frederick and Robert White. On transferring to the steamers they simply became Post Office servants.

The proposal when steam was first approved was to transfer two packets from the Irish services, the *Ivanhoe* and *Meteor,* and to lay down a third, completion of which would enable the sailings to be increased to three times a week. The delay in starting arose partly because of a shortage of vessels on the Irish stations and partly because the two in question needed refitting. The new packet, the *Watersprite,* was ordered in March 1825 and arrived at Weymouth in June the following year, but after a trial crossing to Guernsey was 'borrowed' by Holyhead. In the end it was this vessel which joined the *Ivanhoe* to open the service and which, under the command of Frederick White, carried the first Channel Islands mail to go by steam.

In January 1828 G.H. Freeling, the assistant secretary responsible for packet administration, reported that what he called the 'infant establishment' was functioning satisfactorily, and the Post Office laid down salary and wage rates: for the agent £300 a year - just double his old figure - and for the captains £280. Crew pay ranged from £6 per lunar month for the mate to £3.5.0 for an A.B.[3] It was vainly hoped that these rates, though they were the lowest of any station except

1   *BPP*, 1836, XXVIII, Sixth Report of the Commissioners of Post Office Management, 30 April 1836, Append. B, 11, statement by Captain Hamilton, commander of the Dover steam packet *Ferret.*

2   Abandoned in 1832 in favour of a contract service.

3   *BPP*, 1830, XIV, Append. 18, 5.

Portpatrick, would be high enough to stop smuggling, 'the temptation to which [was] very great at the islands'.[1] Fares were much the same as in the sailing packets and with the change in administration a schedule of rates for horses, carriages &c. was also published, for the first time.[2]

In March 1828 it was decided to introduce the third weekly sailing and to cover this the *Meteor* was transferred from Holyhead, where she had been in reserve. A Weymouth crew were sent to fetch the vessel and their route, by road to Bristol, from there to Dublin by steamer and then back across the Irish Sea by the packet, provides an interesting sidelight on the difficulties of travel before the railways were built. The *Meteor* made her first crossing on 13 April. At about the same time consideration was given to the conveyance by the packets of 'coaching parcels'- i.e. those up to 30lb in weight.[3] The additional sailing was authorised as an experiment, for the summer season and subject to increased earnings more than covering increased costs. In the event they did not do so and from 1829 sailings were again only two, 'one ship to lay up and act as reserve'.[4]

The following year the *Meteor* was wrecked. On the morning of 23 February 1830 she left Guernsey roads with the Weymouth mail, under Lt. Connor, passed the Casquets at 12.30 p.m., in thick haze, and continued on her course at about 7 knots. About 8 o'clock, when near Church Ope, Portland, she went aground. All on board were rescued but as the tide fell a large crowd descended on the wreck and set about looting the passengers' baggage. The mail reached Weymouth overland, at two the following morning.[5] The machinery and gear having been salvaged the wreck was sold, a move that earned reproof for the agent for omitting to obtain the Postmaster General's consent. Because all the Weymouth commanders were related and the agent, William Mackenzie, was not a seaman, the Postmaster General considered it 'most essential' for the official enquiry to be conducted by an outsider, and entrusted the job to Norris Goddard, the agent at Holyhead. No report of the enquiry has survived but the Postmaster General's comments suggest that

1   *BPP*, 1830, XIV, Append. 18, 5.

2   The cabin fare was later reduced to £1.1.0.

3   *BPP*, 1830, XIV. This required the sanction of H.M. Customs. It was already in operation at Holyhead and Milford, the packets there being the only vessels on those passages, and appears to have started at Weymouth shortly afterwards.

4   PO Post 34/17 (Packet Minutes) 264.

5   J M David, 'Early Channel Island steamers, 1823-1840', *Transactions of La Société Guernesiaise'* (1954) 370, and *Dorset County Chronicle*, 25 February 1830.

no very satisfactory conclusion was reached. 'There appears to me to
have been on the part of Captain Connor such a want of due attention
and of judgment', he wrote, 'that I should not feel myself justified
in appointing him to any other pacquet'; and, significantly perhaps,
'the evidence of Captain R. White is very extraordinary and does him
no credit'.[1]

A replacement was ordered the following August and delivered in
July 1831. This was the *Flamer*. She was regarded as a marked
improvement on the older packets but proved in service to be an
indifferent sea-boat, and was often in trouble. Her worst adventure
was in December 1833. On Thursday the 5th she left Weymouth at
midnight under William Roberts, master, deputising for Frederick White.
It was a wicked night and Roberts was immediately forced to put into
Portland roads for shelter. From there, in the morning, he returned to
Weymouth. At 7 o'clock that evening he tried again, and by the following
morning had got as far as Alderney. Some hours later, unable to make any
further headway, he gave up and turned about for Weymouth. At 1 p.m. on
Saturday, more than 36 hours after she had first left, the *Flamer* was
20 miles off the Casquets when she was struck by an outsize wave, which
carried away all the deck gear and the ship's boat and flooded the cabin.
The twelve passengers were driven to huddle together on the companion
ladder, the only dry spot between the waters within and the waters
without. At 3 p.m. on the Sunday she crawled back into Weymouth with
Roberts and five other men seriously injured, one fatally. It was said
that neither of the other packets would have survived such a battering.[2]
Meanwhile, of course, the mail had still not left. It was therefore
transferred to the *Watersprite,* which left on Monday morning only to
return within an hour with a burst boiler. Eventually it reached
Guernsey under sail, in the Weymouth pilot boat.

Although a week's interruption of sailings was not unknown when
conditions were as bad as this the captains had a strong sense of duty,
in the best traditions of the public service, and earned a reputation
for sticking to their schedules through thick and thin. Unfortunately
in their dealings with passengers this same devil-may-care attitude often
got them into trouble, as for instance when Frederick White was
criticised in the island papers for his 'brusque manners'. It appeared
that a passenger on the *Watersprite* had 'had the misfortune, not having
the strength to lift his head from the deck, to soil the bridge a little',
whereupon White let loose on him a 'broadside of insults' and told one of
his men to 'thrust his mop down the dirty fellow's throat'.[3] In Jersey
the packets were unpopular, both with the travelling public, who preferred
the 'private' Southampton steamers, and with the St Helier harbourmaster,
who, as often as not, disregarded their prior rights to certain berths.
The Post Office blamed local financial interests for this 'Southampton
bias' but whatever the reason for it a captain's coarseness could only
aggravate the situation. In 1832 the Postmaster General felt constrained
to issue a strongly worded warning about misbehaviour, remarking 'the

1   PO Post 34/19 (Packet Minutes) 499.

2   David, 'Channel Island steamers', 370, and *Dorset County Chronicle*,
     12 December 1833.

3   David, 'Channel Island steamers', 371.

fact cannot be denied they are exceedingly gross and violent persons'.[1]

Frequent damage and regular complaints reflected administrative shortcomings. The first concern, quite properly, was to deliver the mails but disregard of passenger interests drove traffic away and inflated costs. Many of the packets were out of date, and most were undersized. That did not apply just to Weymouth, of course, but it did apply more forcibly there than elsewhere. The Channel Islands crossing was not only long but, as the Post Office recognised, the most difficult to navigate.

Successive parliamentary committees found much to criticise. In 1830, for instance, the Commissioners of Revenue Inquiry, having investigated all the domestic stations except Dover, reported 'improvident Outlay' on steamers and 'a defective system of Management and Control'.[2] In August 1832 a Select Committee on Post Communication condemned the whole system under which the packets were built and managed by the Post Office and recommended transferring responsibility to the Admiralty.[3]

At Weymouth the packets increasingly lost ground to the Southampton commercial steamers. The latter did not run with the same regularity in winter as in summer and so avoided the worst of the Channel weather, but under the stimulus of competition between rival companies were constantly improved. Better built, better found and better engined than the packets they carried not only more passengers but also, unofficially, many letters, as they provided a quicker transit to and from London. Competition also had its effect on the 'private'fares, which were subjected at times to drastic cutting – at one time to only 2/6 for a deck passage. Though such rates could not last long Southampton fares were consistently lower than those of the packets.[4]

Public concern found an outlet in the island press. Early in 1836, for example, the Guernsey *Comet*,[5] reporting the latest damage to the *Flamer*, commented: 'Since it appears that the Commanders of His Majesty's packets are compelled to put to sea in all weathers we hope that His Majesty's Government will see the necessity of providing larger steamers than those now in use, at least during the winter months ... Not that the Inhabitants of these islands have any cause for complaint relative to the packet service ... that is well executed. But those who are engaged in this service have their lives frequently placed in jeopardy by reason of

1   PO Post 34/24 (Packet Minutes) 29.

2   *BPP*, 1830, XIV, 93.

3   *BPP*, 1832, XVII, 20.

4   David, 'Channel Island steamers', 374.

5   5 February 1836.

the smallness of the vessels with which they are entrusted'.

In April 1836 the Commissioners of Post Office Management, having digested endless evidence on all the domestic stations, concluded that Post Office control was largely ineffectual, everything being left to the local agents. The stations all ran at a loss and management generally was slack, to say the least. Weymouth was a comparatively shining exception. The Commissioners found 'the accounts kept with great regularity and a very efficient and proper control exercised over receipts and expenditure as far as depended on the agent'.[1] The agent at that time was James Agnew Stevens, Lt. R.N., who had previously commanded packets at Falmouth and Holyhead and by his naval training was better qualified to maintain discipline over a seagoing service than most of the other agents. The station showed only a modest annual loss, receipts amounting to 70 per cent of expenditure.[2] Giving evidence before the Commissioners Stevens made the usual recommendations for improving the packets - greater length and greater power - and suggested that thus altered they could easily extend their summer range to St Malo or Granville. The captain of the *Flamer* said that the engines were so weak that in bad weather the packets often lost the tide in Jersey and then had to put back, as there was no safe anchorage near the islands; in fact, in a head sea, 'the wheels could be turned at all only with difficulty'.[3] And Robert White, captain of the *Watersprite*, complained of lack of publicity, saying that he had often brought back to Weymouth passengers who, from such westerly places as Bristol, had gone to the islands via Southampton not realising that any other service existed.[4] Nobody seems to have thought of advertising the packets in post offices. As the Commissioners remarked, except in the ports the public found it very hard to get information about the sailings although notices could have been posted without additional expense in every town and many villages.[5]

A disadvantage peculiar to Weymouth was its distance from Holyhead, where the Post Office dockyard was.[6] Once in about four years each packet was faced with a voyage of over 300 miles, even though there was

1   *BPP*, 1836, XXVIII, 8.

2   Milford by comparison was so inconvenient and little used that the corresponding figure was only 12 per cent. *BPP*, 1836, XXVIII, Append. A, 1.

3   *BPP*, 1836, XXVIII, Append. C, 8, 9, 11, 13.

4   *BPP*, 1836, XXVIII, Append. C, 10. It is difficult to assess the validity of these comments but one feels there may have been a little exaggeration.

5   *BPP*, 1836, XXVIII, 20.

6   Convenient for the Irish packets. Those from Dover went round to the Thames.

a royal dockyard as near as Portsmouth. Nevertheless, the station's management was described as 'highly creditable' to Stevens,[1] and it was felt that if the packets were improved and the mail accelerated Weymouth might become a very efficient station.

Much of the blame for the state of things generally fell on G.H. Freeling, whose defence was that he had been made responsible for far too much. 'I have been anxious for years to get rid of the steam packets, which ought never to have fallen on me ... but did, as fifty other things have done, because there was nobody else to take it up'.[2] Nobody at the Post Office had had professional experience of ships or dockyards. Ever since the introduction of steam the question of contract or establishment had remained open, subject to government decision, and uncertainty about the future militated against improvement within the Post Office.[3] The Postmaster General, the Duke of Richmond, defended Crown ownership because it was 'of the greatest importance ... that the correspondence should not be detained or delayed',[4] and commercial captains could not be expected to thrash their ships through all weathers as the packet commanders did regularly; but the Commissioners were in favour of a contract service or, failing that, transfer to the Admiralty.[5] The Guernsey *Star*, noticing the 1836 report,[6] commented:

> We cannot see the necessity of keeping three crews in constant pay. A packet leaves Weymouth on the Saturday and returns there on Tuesday evening. From that time till the following Wednesday week the crew have absolutely nothing to do. If the Southampton private steamers, which have one-third greater distance to run, can make one voyage weekly in winter and two in summer, and proceed every alternate time to St Malo, the Post Office steamers, if they were improved in speed and power, should be able to make one short voyage per week all the year round. Three *vessels* are needed, one as a stand-by, but not three *crews*.

And, the old familiar complaint; '... the number of passengers would have been considerably greater some years since had the commanders been half as civil as those of the private steamers'.

It is instructive to see the station through the eyes of the man who then had the running of it, Agnew Stevens, writing in October 1836:[7]

1   *BPP*, 1836, XXVIII, 9.

2   *BPP*, 1836, XXVIII Append. H, 9, examination of G.H. Freeling, 7 April 1836.

3   A situation not without its parallels today.

4   *BPP*, 1836, XXVIII, Append. H, 1.

5   *BPP*, 1836, XXVIII, 19.

6   30 June 1836.

7   Letter to Col. W.L. Maberley, who had recently succeeded Francis Freeling as Post Office secretary. PRO Adm. 1/4075.

... there are three Post Office Steam Packets on this Station the state and condition of which is as follows:-

'Watersprite' 186 Tons has been lengthened by the Bow 20ft. which has added to her former Tonnage (162) 24 Tons, she is now receiving additional Steam Power at Blackwall which will give her Engines of about 75 horses power, until she is tried it will be impossible to Report fully on her, but I think that she will prove a fast and efficient Vessel, and as sound as the day she was first launched.

'Flamer' 165 Tons 60 horse power, is only 5 years old, in perfectly good order strong and well built in the bottom but slight and requires strengthening above the waterline, she is too narrow and wants stability in bad weather, is capable when strengthened of receiving the same additional Steam Power as the 'Watersprite', and would then be a fast and, but for her want of stability and body, a fine efficient Vessel.

'Ivanhoe' 185 Tons 60 horse power, was built in 1818[1] and purchased by Government (I believe) in 1822, is very much out of order both in Hull and Machinery from long service, is very slow and in my opinion not worth a general repair.

Until the alterations making in the 'Watersprite' have been tried, it will be impossible to state whether they will render her a fit and proper Vessel for this Station.

In my opinion the Class of Steam Packet here is too small to contend with the heavy Sea and rapid tide met with both about the Norman Islands and the race of Portland, at the same time the shallow water and confined space both in the harbours of St Heliers and Weymouth must of necessity limit their size. Taking all circumstances into consideration I would respectfully submit that about 240 Tons with good Beam and a draft of water not much exceeding 8ft propelled by Engines of 100 horses power would be the kind of Steam Packet best calculated for this Station.

The present Average Passage out & home is about 14 hours which gives a rate of rather under 7 miles an hour. I think that well constructed Packets of the above description would exhibit a rate of 9 miles an hour & thus reduce the average passage by three hours & half.

With this speed the Mail might be dispatched from here during the Summer months at 9 A.M. instead of as at present 9 P.M. and thus expedite its delivery 12 hours, and further that in weather which now stops our present Packets the new ones would Steam ahead 5 or 6 miles an hour. This I would beg leave to observe is no fancied data as the Private Steam Packets 'Atlanta'[2] and 'Lady De Saumarez' have beat the King's Packets full as much.

1   Actually 1820.

2   *Atalanta.*

The Proprietors of these private Packets had two, the 'Beresford'[1] and 'Ariadne' of the same size as ours, and after going to considerable expence in improving them as much as possible they found it necessary to build two of nearly double size in order to keep pace with other Stations and this merely for the conveyance of Passengers.

By a parity of reasoning, so important a duty as the Conveyance of the Mail would still more completely justify the expence of new Packets.

On returning to service, lengthened and re-engined, the *Watersprite* was described by the Guernsey *Star*[2] as 'wonderfully improved in speed'.

As a result of the Commissioners' recommendations a general transfer of responsibility to the Admiralty was ordered, and this took effect on 16 January 1837. Thereafter the Post Office was concerned only with schedules and routes. The civilian commanders of the packets were appointed nominally to H.M.S. *Victory* as 'additional master to command H.M.S. ....'[3] In addition to the commander a master and a pilot were attached to each vessel, and it was commonly assumed that in future the commanders would have an easy time. As the civilian commanders retired they were replaced by serving naval officers.

The Admiralty's first change at Weymouth was to withdraw the *Ivanhoe*. 'Leaky and exhibiting the marks of age' she was sent at the end of January to Woolwich for repairs but on closer inspection was found unfit for further packet service, as Stevens had said, and did not return. In May the other two packets were renamed (a general Admiralty policy), *Flamer* becoming *Fearless* and *Watersprite* becoming *Wildfire*. The *Jersey Times*[4] looked forward to improved vessels as an 'immediate consequence' of the new order but these were not forthcoming. The Treasury no doubt took a different view from Stevens as to the expense being completely justified.

There was, however, an attempt to do something about the existing ones. In September 1837 *Fearless* was sent to Chatham for the strengthening recommended by Stevens and to be fitted with more powerful engines. She was replaced by the Admiralty steam vessel *Pluto*. Rather larger than the regular Weymouth packets this vessel was expected to make the passage to the islands in any weather but in practice her performance appears to have been unremarkable. In fact, she was unpopular. The normal crew of the *Fearless* were unable to handle her and

1   *Lord Beresford* (by now, like the others mentioned, running from Southampton).

2   9 January 1837, quoting the *Jersey Times*.

3   The *Star* (Guernsey) 22 May 1837, quoting the *Devonport Telegraph*.

4   9 January 1837.

extra men had to be hired.

When *Fearless* returned to Weymouth, in January 1838, *Pluto* remained pending delivery of a replacement for the *Ivanhoe,* then being built at Chatham. The new packet, named *Dasher,* was completed in April 1838 and her arrival enabled the *Wildfire* to be taken in hand for hull repairs and reboilering. On her first arrival in Guernsey the *Star* was pleased to note: 'the Dasher appears to be an excellent sea-boat and in good calm weather should reach Weymouth in six hours' - and later added reassuringly 'a newly invented and very elegant lifebuoy hangs over the stern in constant readiness'.[1] Conforming closely to the specification recommended by Stevens the *Dasher* was easily the best packet on the station - but still not really equal to the job. An improvement in November 1838 was the fitting of cycloidal paddle wheels. Afterwards, on trial, she achieved 7½ knots in a cross sea and 9 in calm water, which was considered very satisfactory.

In the summer of 1839 it was decided that *Fearless* was beyond further improvement. With her new engines she could manage 4 knots in a strong head sea, which was better than before, but the increased power was a mixed blessing as she burnt more coal. Extra had to be carried in bags on deck and that in turn aggravated her instability. Reporting favourably on the *Dasher* Stevens considered that 'one other like her' would be enough for a twice-weekly service, and suggested the *Cuckoo,* then lying in reserve at Holyhead.[2] Built in 1824 as the *Cinderella,* for the introduction of steam at Milford, the *Cuckoo* was by this time far from new, but having been at Holyhead Stevens knew what he was getting. She replaced the *Fearless* in August 1839 and after being patched up and repainted took her place alongside the *Dasher* and *Wildfire.* Some time later[3] the *Dorset County Chronicle* could still describe her as 'replete with every comfort' and 'unsurpassed by any other packet'.

From May 1840 the Southampton steamers enjoyed the benefit of the opening of the London and South Western Railway, which brought that port to within about three hours of London. It was not long before letters were being sent that way with the Post Office's blessing, provided that they were endorsed 'by private steamer' or 'via Southampton'. The quicker transit by that route revived the possibility of Southampton becoming the official mail station, already rumoured while the railway was being built,and in 1841 the Admiralty appointed a committee to look into the question.[4] They conceded that Southampton was quicker to London,

1   19 and 26 April 1838.

2   PRO Adm. 1/4067, 27 June 1839.

3   11 January 1844.

4   Committee appointed ... to inquire as to the comparative advantages offered by different ports in the Channel as ports for the arrival and departure of the Channel Islands mails, 25 March 1841 (Blue Books 1841, XXVI).

by about two hours, but considered that on balance the advantage still lay with Weymouth - commercially because it was nearer Falmouth, and therefore more convenient for Jersey's overseas mails, and navigationally for reasons already well known. In particular, they pointed out, a direct course from Weymouth took a vessel well clear of the Casquets whereas Southampton vessels had to set a careful course to avoid that hazard. Crossing to Jersey in the *Dasher* they found her 'deficient in power' and recommended three new packets each of 400 tons and 180 horsepower, to run three times a week. Greater power was considered desirable not so much for increased speed as for greater reliability.

It was all too late. The absence from the report of any specific reference to the railway suggests that its significance had been underestimated. Casquets or no Casquets, it was with Southampton that the real advantage now lay. In 1843 the London and South Western joined forces with the Southampton steamer companies to form the South Western Steam Packet Company, and the resulting integration of rail and sea produced a service that Weymouth could not match. Later that year the Post Office began to use Southampton instead of Falmouth for many overseas mails, which weakened the case for Weymouth packets, and early in 1844 it emerged that a contract was being negotiated for the Channel Islands mails to go that way also.

The end came on 26 April 1845, when the *Cuckoo* brought the mail into Weymouth for the last time and the outward mail went from Southampton. The *Dasher* and *Wildfire* had already left for Woolwich to pay off, before taking up naval duties elsewhere, and a few days later the *Cuckoo* followed.

III

Having seen why and how the Weymouth packet service began, and something of how it was conducted, we may perhaps conclude with a few words about its impact on the port itself and in the islands.

Like most small ports with a long history Weymouth has had its ups and downs. After the town had been badly damaged during the Civil War, and again in 1665, by fire, most of the old harbour trade decayed and recovery was very slow. By 1794, however, when the packet station was established, things were improving. The additional source of employment offered by the packets was no doubt welcome. Though limited it was regular, and if the pay was poor the service did at least confer the benefit of freedom from impressment.

The harbour itself at that time was in a run-down state, after years of neglect, and arrangements for the packets appear to have been limited to the provision of moorings. One was near the entrance, at a spot called the Old Hole, where they could lie at anchor in deep water sheltered from the south-west by a small promontory called the Nothe, and the other in Portland roads.

Except to those actually involved the packets were initially of no great consequence to Weymouth - as far as can be judged from what is admittedly for the most part negative evidence. Contemporary newspapers,

for instance, offer no more than the occasional passing mention. With
the passing of the years, however, they became more important. By the
early 1800s they were included in all the local guide books, and there
must have been increasing 'spin-off' for local trade; for hoteliers
from passengers in transit as well as more obviously for chandlers and
storekeepers. Four of the packets were built in a local yard, if not
in Weymouth itself at least within the limits of the port, at Portland
- the *Chesterfield* of 1806, the *Francis Freeling*, the second
Chesterfield, of 1812, and the *Countess of Liverpool*.

From the 1820s onward the local press regularly recorded arrivals
and sailings, and the wrecks of the *Hinchinbrook* and *Freeling* were
reported in some detail. The latter had a profound effect on the town.
A local disaster fund was set up for dependants, which may have
influenced the Postmaster General's decision to grant them an annual
allowance - though that was not without precedent.

In Jersey and Guernsey the impact was more immediate, as was only
to be expected, and within a very short time, as already mentioned, the
packets had become indispensable, particularly to island commerce.
They also helped to establish the tourist trade, so important today.[1]
As well as establishing the packets the Act of 1794 instituted British
post offices in Jersey and Guernsey, and the islands' French
orientation, disrupted by the Napoleonic wars, was afterwards much less
pronounced.[2]

The coming of steam to the packet service was greeted with general
acclaim. Not only were special berths appointed for their use in both
Weymouth and Jersey, but in Weymouth other vessels were prohibited from
mooring in any part of the harbour where their anchors or buoys would
obstruct the passage of the packets.[3] Local labour profited rather
more than before from the carrying out of small repairs and local
tradesmen from supplying stores. At first some stores were bought by
the captains in Jersey but after the appointment of Stevens as agent,
in 1833, everything was bought in Weymouth by contract, including coal.[4]
Weymouth, in fact, was very proud of its steam packets, and the press
reported not only their movements but their performance generally. It

1   Not everybody was pleased. In 1799 we find the Rev Mr Gibert, of
    Guernsey, objecting to the packet arriving on Sunday, and
    scandalised at the distribution of letters and newspapers during
    the hours of divine service. PO E685K/1814, XXXIX.

2   They remained part of the U.K. postal system until 1 October 1969,
    becoming independent when the Post Office became a public
    corporation instead of a department of state.

3   Geo.A Ellis, *History of Weymouth and Melcombe Regis* (1829) p.95.

4   *BPP*, 1836, XXVIII, 8.

was some years before any other steam vessels used the port regularly and there was no steamer on the Weymouth register until 1840.[1]

The impending closure of the packet service was viewed with dismay, and a deputation waited on the Chancellor of the Exchequer in the hope of averting it. The Weymouth press became unashamedly partisan, constantly - and quite unfairly - disparaging the Southampton steamers while writing up any good performance by one of the packets. When the end came the mayor and leading citizens presented Robert White, the longest-serving commander, with a farewell testimonial. In the islands, too, the captains' 'brusque manners' presumably forgiven, or forgotten, there were numerous objections to closure and for some time afterwards much complaint about the Southampton service.

The Weymouth Post Office packets spanned barely more than 51 years, but it would be a mistake to conclude that they had no lasting significance. Quite the contrary. Their withdrawal was cited in evidence in support of the Wilts. Somerset and Weymouth Railway bill, just then before Parliament; in 1848 Post Office wishes secured the inclusion in the London and South Western Railway's Steam Vessels Act[2] of powers to run from Weymouth; and, when the railway did eventually reach the town, influential support for the reopening of the route came from Agnew Stevens, then living in retirement in Jersey.

Under railway management the route was reopened in April 1857, on ordinary commercial lines, and in the course of time the harbour trade became a major source of employment and an important factor in the town's economy. The cross-channel steamers have remained the mainstay of that trade, and successive harbour developments have all been geared to their needs. It can be argued, in short, that had it not become a packet station Weymouth would in time have irrevocably declined, in the way of so many small ports. In the event it still prospers, on foundations laid by the packets.[3]

1   The *Rose*.

2   11 & 12 Vic c.125.

3   The subsequent history of the Weymouth cross-channel services is discussed in the author's *The Great Western at Weymouth* (Newton Abbot: David & Charles, 1971). That account and the present one may be regarded as complementary to one another.

SOURCES USED:

Material covering the years 1794 to 1837 is drawn mainly from the records of the Post Office (held at London Postal Headquarters, St. Martin's Le Grand).

Treasury Books	Post 1
Packet Minutes	Post 34
P.M.G's Minutes	Post 35
Packet Reports	Post 41
Freeling's Minutes	Post 42
E 685K/1814 (on Channel Island posts generally)	

Correspondence covering the Admiralty period is preserved at the Public Record Office, Adm. 1/4066-7 and 4075-6.

British Parliamentary Papers *(BPP)*:

Twenty-second Report of the Commissioners of Inquiry into the Collection and Management of the Revenue arising in Ireland and Great Britain (Post Office Revenue, United Kingdom) Part V, Packet Establishment, Home Stations, 25 June 1830, *BPP,* 1830, XIV.
Sixth Report of the Commissioners appointed to inquire into the Management of the Post Office Department, 30 April 1836, *BPP,* 1836, XXVIII.

Various West Country and Channel Island newspapers (as mentioned in the footnotes).

APPENDIX 1

(a) Channel Islands Post Office packets on the Weymouth register
(measurements to nearest inch : tonnages to nearest ton)

EARL OF CHESTERFIELD (16/1795); sq. sterned clench built cutter;
56'0" x 19'0" x 9'0", 78 tons;
built by Bools & Good, Bridport, 1795; broken up 1811.

ROVER (30/1799); sq. sterned cutter, 53'0" x 8'9", 67 tons;
built at West Cowes, 1789; broken up 1813.

CHESTERFIELD (32/1806); sq. sterned cutter with flush deck;

58'4" x 18'11" x 9'5", 85 tons;

built by Thos. Ayles, Portland, 1806; taken prize 1811.

GENERAL DOYLE (19/1807); sq. sterned clench built cutter;

57'8" x 19'3" x 9'0", 83 tons;

built at Looe, 1803; registered de novo, Guernsey, 1810.

FRANCIS FREELING (25/1809); sq. sterned carvel built cutter with flush deck;

57'7" x 19'4" x 9'2", 86 tons;

built by Thos. Ayles, Portland, 1809; lost 1826.

HINCHINBROOK (13/1811); sq. sterned carvel built cutter with flush deck;

60'0" x 19'8" x 10'0", 90 tons;

built by Wm. Good, Bridport, 1811; lost 1826.

CHESTERFIELD (23/1812); sq. sterned carvel built cutter with flush deck;

63'4" x 20'0" x 10'1", 107 tons;

built by Thos. Ayles, Portland, 1812; registered de novo, Southampton, 1818.

COUNTESS OF LIVERPOOL (2/1814); sq. sterned cutter with flush deck;

62'2" x 20'1" x 10'3", 104 tons;

built by Thos. Ayles, Portland, 1813; sold to Postmaster General, 1828.*

Source: Weymouth Shipping Registers

(b) Weymouth Post Office and Admiralty steam packets

IVANHOE: 103'9" x 16'9" x 11'3", 158 tons; built 1820 by J. Scott & Sons, Greenock; bought by Post Office 1821 for £4425 after running privately; at Holyhead and Milford until 1826, then refitted and re-engined for Weymouth at cost of nearly £8000; withdrawn from packet service 1837; broken up about 1841 as H.M.S. BOXER.

*   when sailing packets were displaced by steam it was Post Office practice to buy them in. The *Countess of Liverpool* was bought for £1677 and later resold for £600.

WATERSPRITE: 107'0" x 17'2" x 11'8", 162 tons; built 1826 by Geo. Graham, Harwich; cost £9658; renamed WILDFIRE, 1837; at Weymouth until closure of station; lasted on minor naval and yard duties until 1888.

METEOR: 190 tons (no record of dimensions); built 1821 by Wm. Evans, Rotherhithe, for introduction of steam at Holyhead; cost £8921; afterwards at Milford; transferred to Weymouth 1828; wrecked 1830.

FLAMER: 111'0" x 17'0" x 11'4", 165 tons; built 1831 by Fletcher, Son & Fearnall, Limehouse, to replace METEOR; cost £7190; renamed FEARLESS, 1837; withdrawn from packet service 1839; on minor naval and yard duties until 1875.

DASHER: 120'0" x 21'8" x 13'0", 260 tons; built 1838 at Chatham; cost £11327; replacement for IVANHOE; at Weymouth until closure of station; afterwards on Channel Islands fishery protection; broken up 1885.

CUCKOO: 119'6" x 19'8" x 12'6", 234 tons; built 1824 by Wigram & Green, Blackwall, for introduction of steam at Milford; cost £10615; later at Holyhead; until 1837 named CINDERELLA; transferred to Weymouth 1839 to replace FEARLESS and remained until closure of station; afterwards on Channel Islands fishery protection; broken up 1864.

PLUTO: 135'0" x 24'0" x 11'10", 365 tons; built at Chatham, 1831; Admiralty steam vessel used as temporary packet for about 6 months, 1837/8.

The building costs quoted were divided roughly 55 per cent for the hull and 45 per cent for the engines.

Sources: the particulars in this list have been taken from several sources, notably the 1830 and 1836 Parliamentary reports already referred to, the Post Office Packet Minutes and Packet Reports, and *List of the Navy* (not to be confused with the Navy List) in the Naval Library, Ministry of Defence.

APPENDIX 2

Establishment of the Weymouth packets, 1794

General Post Office.

February 3, 1794

Notice is hereby given that a Packet will sail every Thursday from Weymouth for the Islands of Guernsey and Jersey, and a Mail with the Letters for these Islands will be made and sent from this Office every Wednesday Night. The First Mail is to sail if possible on Thursday the 6th Instant.

The Course the Packet will take, and the Times of her Stay and Return, will be in general, and, unless in Cases of particular and occasional Orders to the contrary, the same as in the last War, namely, to sail to Guernsey and drop her Letters there, to proceed immediately to Jersey, there to deliver her Letters, and to stay Three Days for the Answers, then to return to Guernsey, deliver her Letters, stay there Two Days, and return to Weymouth.

By Command of the Postmaster General. Anth. Todd, Sec.

Source: *London Gazette,* February 1794.

APPENDIX 3

Auction of a Weymouth packet, 1806

WEYMOUTH

To be SOLD by AUCTION, by T. TINDALL, on Tuesday the
Ninth of December, at the King's Head Inn, - THE EARL
OF CHESTERFIELD PACKET, lately in the service of his
Majesty, in conveying the mail from Weymouth to the
Islands of Guernsey & Jersey; has great accommodations,
and may be sent to sea at a small expence.

DIMENSIONS

	ft.	ins.
Length aloft	56	0¾
Breadth	19	0
Height in the hold	9	1½

Admeasures 77 82-94th Tons

Was built by Mess. Bools and Good, Bridport, all with
1½ inch oak; is particularly calculated for a Packet,
or any other purpose where dispatch is required.

For particulars, apply to T. Tindall, broker, Weymouth.
The sale to begin at three o'clock in the afternoon.

Source: *Salisbury & Winchester Journal*, 1 December 1806.

APPENDIX 4

General orders for the Weymouth packets, 1813

GENERAL ORDERS

To the Commanders of His Majesty's Packet Boats on the Weymouth Station.

1. On or before the morning of your turn to be on duty, or that the Service may require you to be so, your Packet Boat, with all her Crew on board, must be *afloat,* and in a situation so as to be free to sail when necessary, and within half an hour after the arrival of the Mail from London, your Gunner and one other trusty person of your Crew must be waiting at the Post Office to receive the Mails for Guernsey and Jersey, and then to convey them *immediately* on board your Packet Boat, by which time you and your Master are each required to be there also.

2. As soon as the Mails are on board you are to secure them from Wet or other Injury, and make fast the proper weights to them, so as to be ready to sink them if necessary to prevent their falling into the hands of the enemy, for which you will be responsible - And whenever the Mail Portmanteaus may be delivered to you unlocked, or unsealed, or otherwise imperfectly secured, you are to report the same to me by the first opportunity.

3. You are allowed one hour only after the arrival of the Mail from London for getting the Passengers and their luggage on board your vessel, at the expiration of which time you must sail, wind and weather permitting.

4. Whenever the state of wind and tide is such as to prevent your Sailing at the appointed time you are nevertheless to remain on board your vessel, and not suffer any of your Crew to leave it, so that you may proceed to sea, the moment the circumstances will allow you.

5. Whenever the state of the weather is so adverse as to make it obviously dangerous for you to attempt to sail, or to go on board at the appointed time you must state the circumstances to me in writing to be forwarded to the Postmaster General, and upon such occasions when you have leave to wait a more favourable tide, you are nevertheless to continue in readiness to start at a moment's notice; and you must proceed to sea as soon as the weather moderates, without waiting for any further order to do so.

6. You are on no account to sail without your Boat, or to encumber your Deck, or to omit the constant use of your Waistcloths, Nettings and Ridge Chains; and you are to take especial care that your Gunner keeps the arms of every description and the ammunition in perfect order for use, and ready at all times for my inspection, and you will once at least in every fortnight exercise your Crew at the great Guns and small arms.

7. You are to commence your Journal by noting down the exact time at which you receive the Mails from the Post Office, and at which you get under weigh, and if you are prevented Sailing immediately on your going on board, or within the appointed time you are to assign sufficient reason in your Journal for such delay.

8. You are to avoid as much as possible any other delay at Guernsey, than what may be necessary for the landing or receiving the Mails or passengers at that Island; and you are to remain three days at Jersey, counting the day of arrival one, the next day and the day of sailing the third, always taking your departure from Jersey as early as possible on the morning of the third day.

9. Whenever you make Guernsey, or Jersey, or Weymouth, without being able to sail at once into their respective harbors, you are therefore to take the Mails on Shore in your own Boat, without waiting till the vessel can be brought to her Moorings and on all occasions you are to consider the safety and dispatch of H.M. Mails and Expresses, as the principal objects of your care, and to use the greatest possible exertion in the conveyance and delivery of them to the Place of their destination.

10. As often as you return to this Port or whenever you are prevented first making it, and judge it for the advantage of the Public Service to land the Mails at any other place, you are in either case to report to me immediately such arrival.

11. As soon as possible after your return to this Port, you are to furnish me with a fair Copy of your Log Book, and a list of all your Passengers to and from the Islands, distinguishing Whole, Half or Free, accompanied by a Proper Certificate for the latter.

12. On the arrival and sailing of your Packet Boat at or from this Port, you are always to hold your Crew in readiness to be mustered on board at such hours as from time to time I may appoint.

13. You are not to discharge, or suffer any of your Crew to quit the Service, till the usual protection from Impress has been returned to me, for the purpose of being cancelled, and before you engage any new Seaman, you are first to assure me in writing (if required) that he is qualified for the service.

14. You are not permitted to remain on Shore during the voyage of your Packet Boat without leave of absence from the Postmaster General and whenever you obtain permission to remain on Shore, you must submit to me the person whom you intend to command the vessel in your absence, who must have attained the age of 21 years, and have been 8 years at Sea, and in case of the necessary absence of any of your Crew, the person intended as a substitute must always be submitted to my approval.

15. You are not to make or suffer to be made any private Collection of Letters, either by your Seamen or Passengers and you are to make known

to them, that they will incur a penalty of five pounds for every Letter so conveyed, and that any of your Crew so offending will be for ever dismissed the Service of the Post Office and be turned over to H.M. Navy.

16. In all cases, the Packet Boat first arriving at her Moorings in Weymouth harbour, is to take the first turn of duty from thence to the Islands, and when two Packet Boats arrive the same tide at Weymouth, one having a Mail on board and the other without, that which conveyed the Mail is to take the first turn; and if both had Mails on board, then the first turn is to be taken by the one which conveyed the Mail of the oldest date; and if neither had a Mail on board then the first turn is to be taken by the one that first left Weymouth.

17. Whenever there are two Packet Boats in Harbor together at Guernsey or Jersey, each homewards bound, the one that first arrived there, must sail immediately with or without a Mail; and whenever there are three Packet Boats in any of the said Harbors, all homewards bound, then the first two in like manner must sail immediately.

18. Whenever a Packet Boat may be wanted for any special Service, at any time not in the usual course of sailing, the one first in turn for duty must nevertheless proceed thereon immediately, and the one next in turn must prepare and hold herself in readiness to sail when necessary.

19. Whenever a Vessel is hired for the Public Service, owing to any neglect or disobedience of orders on the part of any Commander, all Expenses so incurred, will be deducted from the hire of his Packet Boat, and he will also be held answerable to the Postmaster General for his misconduct.

20. Whenever a Packet Boat requires to go into Dock, or to be hauled up for the purpose of refitting, a special report in writing must be made of the same; and the Commander must provide a fit vessel to perform the Service, or the Hire of his Packet Boat will be stopped, till she is reported to be again ready for duty.

21. You are to deliver to me at the end of every Quarter, a Return of all the Passengers, Carriages, Horses, Bullion &c. conveyed by your Packet Boat within that period, and also the Quarterly Accounts of your Seamen's wages, with their receipts - these several Accounts must be so drawn out that you may attest them on oath if necessary.

22. Whenever you have occasion to communicate officially with the General Post Office you are to transmit the Letter or Document, unsealed through me, and whenever any new order is issued, each Commander will be furnished with a Copy of it, which he will be held responsible for the execution of without further Directions.

By Command of His Majesty's Postmaster General

Agent

Weymouth, 1813

Source: abstract from Packet Service Instructions (Orders to Officers at
        Home and Abroad re. Foreign Mails &c. 1812-1848), PO E685K/1814, XLIX.

APPENDIX 5

Number of passengers &c.

conveyed between Weymouth and Guernsey and Jersey, 1833-5

Year	Passengers	Carriages	Horses	Dogs	Parcels	Bullion
1833*	4587	5	9	64	337	nil
1834	7866	9	14	97	528	nil
1835	7218	4	16	83	634	nil

*period 26 April to 31 December only

Source: *BPP*, 1836, XXVIII, Append. C, 6.

H.M. Post Office steam packet *Flamer* entering Weymouth harbour, c.1831

HIS MAJESTY'S POST OFFICE

STEAM PACKETS.

One of these Packets with the Mails and Passengers, leaves Weymouth for the Islands of GUERNSEY and JERSEY, every Wednesday and Saturday, at 9 o'clock, P. M. weather permitting, and leaves the Islands for Weymouth, every Tuesday and Saturday, the time being dependant on the tides.

RATES OF PASSAGE MONEY.

Cabin Passengers, each	£1	1	0
Female Servants, each	0	15	0
Male Servants, each	0	12	6

Children under Ten years of age, to be charged half the rates paid by their Parents.

Carriages with Four Wheels, each	3	0	0
Ditto, Two Wheels, each	1	10	0
Horses, each	1	10	0
Dogs, with their Owners, each	0	2	6
Ditto, on Freight, each	0	5	0
Parcels of or under 30lbs. weight	0	2	6
Cash or Bullion, per Thousand Pounds	1	1	0

The above Rates to be paid in British Money, and the Freight of all Parcels must be paid for at the time they are received on board.

These Packets possess every accommodation for Passengers, are remarkably fine Vessels, and the Captains Gentlemen of great skill in their profession.

RESIDENT AGENT,
CAPT. J. AGNEW STEVENS, R. N.
COMMANDERS,
Capt. ROBERT WHITE, *Watersprite*,
Capt. LIVEING, *Flamer*,
Capt. COMBEN, *Ivanhoe*.

Advertisement in Commin's *New Weymouth Guide*, 1835

Packet at her mooring,
in entrance to Weymouth
harbour, c.1825

Packet at her mooring (the Nothe in background) c.1825

Instructions, No. II, 1845.

By Command of the Postmaster General.

NOTICE TO THE PUBLIC,

AND

Instructions to all Postmasters, Sub-Postmasters, and Letter Receivers.

GENERAL POST OFFICE,
April, 1845.

On and after the 26th instant, the Mails for the **CHANNEL ISLANDS** will be conveyed from *Southampton* instead of from Weymouth as at present.

The Mails will be made up and dispatched from Southampton on the *Evenings* of *Tuesday, Thursday,* and *Saturday.*

Post Office notice on withdrawal of Weymouth packets, April 1845

HIS MAJESTY's STEAM PACKET Watersprite,

R. WHITE, Commander,

Will leave this for GUERNSEY & WEYMOUTH on the day , 183 , at o'Clock

☞ PASSENGERS ARE REQUESTED TO BE IN TIME.

JERSEY, the day of 183

COMMINS, PRINTER, LIBRARY, ESPLANADE, WEYMOUTH.

Jersey sailing notice, for completion in manuscript

THE TRADE AND SHIPPING OF MORWELLHAM IN THE NINETEENTH CENTURY

Amber Patrick

During much of the nineteenth century Morwellham was one of the most important quays on the river Tamar. Its growth during that century was largely due to the copper mines in the Tavistock area of south-west Devon, in particular Devon Great Consols. Most of the copper produced was sent to South Wales via Morwellham and the quay's prosperity without doubt rested on the copper trade. As well as shipments out the quay also handled supplies of coal and other materials for the mines and the surrounding districts. This paper considers the trades which contributed to Morwellham's prosperity in the nineteenth century and the vessels involved in such commerce.

II

Morwellham is on the western edge of Devonshire, being on the eastern bank of the Tamar, the largest river in Devon and Cornwall. The quay is eighteen miles upstream from Plymouth and two miles below Weir Head. It is thus on the tidal and navigable part of the river, but close to the upper limit of both. By land the quay is four miles south-west of the stannary town of Tavistock and is one and a half miles south-east of Gunnislake. Morwellham's main rival quays were downstream: Newquay and Gawton on the Devonshire side of the river and Calstock on the Cornish side.

Morwellham was in existence by the mid-thirteenth century, the date of its earliest documentary reference, and even by then the quay appears to have been well established.[1] At this time and later, until the dissolution of the monasteries, the quay primarily served Tavistock Abbey. A variety of goods would have been imported, including wine, cider, and sea sand, with fish a most important item as the Abbey's Benedictine order was non-meat eating. Among the exports tin was almost certainly notable. The early medieval period saw a boom in tin production in south-west Devon, and no doubt that coined at Tavistock was shipped away via Morwellham, but there is no documentary proof of this. Nothing is known about the vessels which carried these goods. The earliest known reference to ships at the quay is in John Leland's *Itinerary:* 'And Shippes cum up within a Mile of this Bridg [New Bridge at Gunnislake] to a Place caullid Morleham [Morwellham]'.[2] Leland's visit to the south-west was made between 1534 and 1543, and it would seem that by this date Morwellham was a shipping place of at least some local importance.

1   Herbert P R Finberg, *West country historical studies* (Newton Abbot: David & Charles, 1969).

2   Richard P Chope, ed. *Early tours in Devon and Cornwall* (Newton Abbot: David & Charles, 1967) p.52.

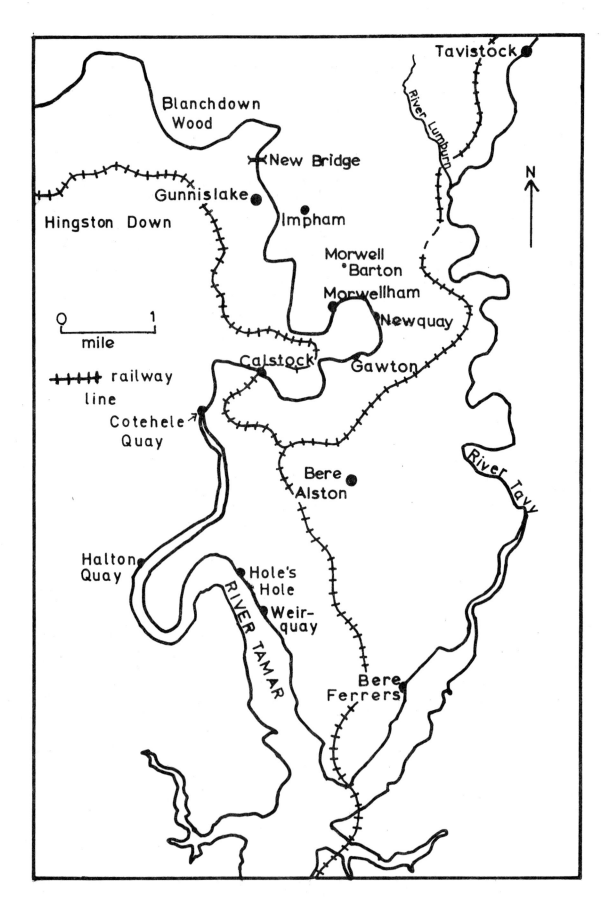

Figure 1 The Tamar Valley.

In 1539 most of the Tavistock Abbey lands, including Morwellham, were granted to the Russell family, who later became Dukes of Bedford. Until the eighteenth century there is little surviving evidence to indicate how rapidly Morwellham and its trade developed. What evidence there is suggests that the quay's trade expanded in the second half of the seventeenth century, stagnated during the mid-eighteenth century, but began to expand again in the 1790s. Certainly it was not until 1790 that the quay's facilities were improved.[1] Shipping is also sparsely documented with no references to it in connection with Morwellham until the middle of the eighteenth century. Then three vessels are mentioned with regard to the quay, the *Morwellham Trader,* the *William and Rebecca,* and the *Southampton.* There are also references to the importation of sea sand in barges to Morwellham.[2]

Prosperity really came to the quay in the nineteenth century, with the increasing production of copper ore in the surrounding area. In the early decades of the century the most productive mines were Wheal Crebor on the Tavistock Canal and Wheals Crowndale and Friendship.[3] The latter was in Mary Tavy parish. Their output, however, was far exceeded by Devon Great Consols, which opened in 1844 and finally closed in 1901, although it was no longer producing copper by then.[4] In the 1850s and 1860s it produced unprecedentedly large quantities of copper ore, most of which was exported via Morwellham, although some was sent out through Newquay and Gawton. Devon Great Consols produced so much copper ore that by 1857 it became worthwhile to build a new dock and quays at Morwellham, while a railway was constructed between the quays and the mine. The new dock and quays greatly improved the shipping facilities and were the final phase in Morwellham's expansion. Not many years later buildings were being demolished. In its heyday (see Figure 2) Morwellham's shipping facilities included the Devon Consols dock and quay complex, the dock in front of the manganese store, the quay between this dock and the canal dock, a small quay in front of the lime kilns and the old copper ore quay beneath the ore chutes.[5] The canal dock was in fact the one reputed to date back to medieval times: it served the inclined plane which connected it to the Tavistock Canal. This canal had been built between 1803 and 1817 and ran from Tavistock, through Morwell Down to end 240 feet above Morwellham. The inclined plane then linked it with the medieval dock, and a branch line also served the top of the ore chutes.

As for the remainder of Morwellham's history, economic decline had set in by the late 1860s. In 1873 the Tavistock Canal closed and was sold

1   Devon County Record Office (DRO) L1258, Letter F, Bundle 118.

2   DRO W1258 LP 1/3; W1258 LP 9/3 and L1258, Letter A, Nos. 17 and 18.

3   DRO L1258, Accounts G, Nos. 60a-88b, and Canals, Tavistock No. 1.

4   J C Goodridge, 'Devon Great Consols: a study of a Victorian mining enterprise', *Transactions of the Devonshire Association*, 96 (1964) 228-68.

5   DRO T1258 E39, Annual Report for 1867.

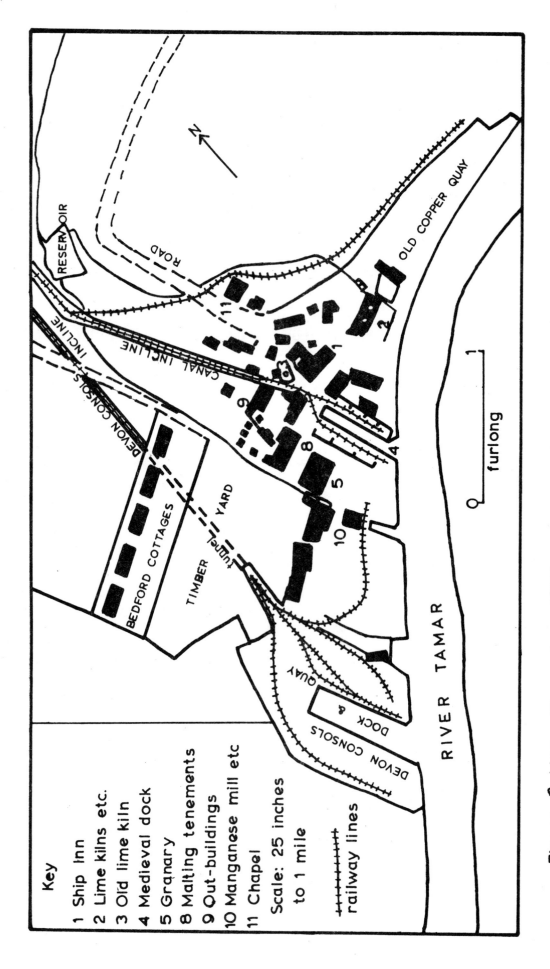

Key

1 Ship Inn
2 Lime kilns etc.
3 Old lime kiln
4 Medieval dock
5 Granary
8 Malting tenements
9 Out-buildings
10 Manganese mill etc
11 Chapel

Scale: 25 inches to 1 mile

++++++ railway lines

RESERVOIR

ROAD

OLD COPPER QUAY

INCLINE

CANAL INCLINE

DEVON CONSOLS

BEDFORD COTTAGES

TIMBER YARD

Tunnel

DEVON CONSOLS

DOCK 4 QUAY

RIVER TAMAR

furlong

N

Figure 2 Morwellham circa 1867.

back to the Duke of Bedford. The 1870s and 1880s saw a steady decline in copper production and therefore in Morwellham's trade and shipping. The only commodity in which production did not decline rapidly was arsenic. By the 1890s very few sailing vessels needed to call at the quay and when Devon Great Consols finally closed in 1901, trading ceased.

Although copper was the most important commodity to pass through the quay, there was a substantial trade in other goods. Large quantities of coal were imported for the mines and for the iron foundries in Tavistock, while culm (poor quality coal) was imported to burn the limestone, yet another imported commodity. The burnt lime was in demand as a manure and for building mortar and lime washing. A variety of timber was also imported. Other minerals exported were lead, tin, manganese and arsenic. Some timber was also exported.

III

Morwellham was, and is, part of the Port of Plymouth,[1] and in the nineteenth century came within the limits of Plymouth's sub-port of Calstock. Unfortunately this low placing within the port hierarchy has meant that very few official records mention Morwellham's trade and shipping, even at the height of the quay's prosperity. Only occasionally are there mentions of vessels calling at the quay in the Custom House Plymouth, Collector to Board, Letter Books. The Plymouth Registers of Shipping, however, provide valuable information on the details of individual vessels, and they indicate which locally-owned ships had Morwellham owners. Other information on the quay's shipping activities comes from the local newspapers, in particular the *Tavistock Gazette,* which provides the most detailed information on vessels. Also of use are the papers of various South Wales copper smelting companies, but without doubt the most important source is the Bedford Tavistock Estate Papers. Those relating to the Tavistock Canal and the various accounts have proved most useful for tracing Morwellham's maritime activities.

In the nineteenth century Morwellham's trade involved both coasting vessels and Tamar barges. Undoubtedly the former were engaged in transporting the more profitable cargoes, but the barge trade was an important one, especially in respect of the number of vessels involved. The barge trade will be considered first.

The commodity most commonly imported by barge was limestone. It came from the quarries around Plymouth, and some probably came from those at Pomphlett, which were owned by the Duke of Bedford and leased to Messrs Gill and Rundle. Members of these two families were the lessees of Morwellham from 1791 to 1854, and had shares in the Tavistock Canal. No complete record of the quantities of limestone imported via Morwellham has survived for the nineteenth century, but the monthly accounts of the

1   Public Record Office (PRO) E 178, D 2860.

Tavistock Canal give some idea of the quantities brought to the quay
and sent along the canal between 1817 and 1869.[1] The quantities imported for the canal ranged from as low as 354 tons in 1817, the year
in which the canal opened, and when most of the limestone appears to
have been burnt at Morwellham and then sent along the canal as lime,
to as high as 9862 tons in 1819. Usually, however, between 3000 and
5000 tons were imported annually for the canal. Of course, limestone
would have been imported for burning at Morwellham itself. Unfortunately, the only source for the amounts of limestone imported, other
than for the canal, are the Duke of Bedford's accounts. These only
give figures for the 1850s and 1860s and from these it would appear
that the quantities of limestone sent along the canal were usually just
over half the total quantity imported.[2] It is, however, likely that in
the earlier years of the century rather more limestone was imported for
burning at the quay.

The evidence on the barges bringing the limestone is rather thin
and comes only from the records of the Tavistock Canal.[3] Usually the
dues payable on the limestone were stated, annually, in a lump sum, but
for the years 1867-9 the names of the barges, the amount they brought
and the dues payable were noted, although the Canal records are only
complete for 1868 (see Table 1).

Table 1

Number of vessels bringing limestone to Morwellham
for the Tavistock Canal, 1867-9

	1867	1868	1869
January	NR	6	14
February	NR	15	16
March	NR	19	19
April	20	13	22
May	14	7	0
June	9	13	0
July	2	0	0
August	4	11	0
September	3	7	0
October	11	7	NR
November	6	12	NR
December	0	11	NR

NR - no record

1   DRO L1258, Canals, Tavistock No. 1.

2   DRO T1258, West Country rentals for 1855 to 1870.

3   DRO L1258, Canals, Tavistock Nos. 26, 27, 28 and 29.

In that year 121 barges brought 4700 tons of limestone. This figure simply totals the amount brought by each barge, and agrees with the figures in the main Canal tonnage accounts. (The general accounts for the rest of the quay do not, at this date, record the quantities of goods passing through Morwellham, only the dues paid). However, if the general proportion of the total quantities of limestone imported by the Tavistock Canal was as in the years for which the figures do survive, it is likely that just over one hundred barges additionally brought limestone to Morwellham, other than for the canal. Thus the total number of barges which came with limestone to the quay in 1868 was probably between 200 and 220, and this in a year when the trade of both the quay and the canal was declining. In more prosperous years it is likely that 250 or more barges were engaged in Morwellham's limestone trade. Certainly in 1819 that number of barges alone would have been required to bring the limestone carried along the canal, assuming that the size of the cargoes carried by the barges was similar to those whose capacity is known for the late 1860s. Also, of course, in 1819 there would have been the barges supplying Morwellham's own limekilns. This indicates that well over 300 barges may have been involved in the quay's limestone trade in the years of peak activity.

The Canal dues returns indicate that twenty-six different barges brought limestone in 1867, 1868 and 1869, and it has been possible to trace fifteen of them. All were registered at Plymouth, and were fairly locally, although not Morwellham, owned at the time they appear in the Plymouth Shipping Registers. Of particular interest is the *Tavistock*,[1] her owners being Messrs Gill and Rundle, merchants of Tavistock. Gill was also a banker, and although neither individual was one of the lessees of Morwellham, they were probably closely related to them, by family and business connections. In fact Messrs Gill and Rundle had shares in five barges as early as 1825 (the pre-1824 Shipping Registration Act registers have not survived). Four of these vessels they came to own completely, the *Good Intent*,[2] the *Glory*, the *Industry* and the *Tavistock*, and they had a majority shareholding in the *Morwellham*.[3] The barges were kept for varying lengths of time: the *Glory* was sold in 1836, and the *Morwellham* may have been lost about the same time, as she is not mentioned in *Lloyd's Register* after that date. The other three were kept until the 1860s: the *Good Intent* being sold in 1861, the *Industry* in 1867 and the *Tavistock* in 1870, the year in which the last recorded importation of limestone at Morwellham occurred. Certainly the Gills - one of whom had become the sole owner of the barges in 1854, the date of the expiry of the Morwellham lease and the time at which Rundle left the partnership - had almost ceased to do business at the quay by 1870. As for the *Tavistock*, she appears regularly in the Canal dues returns for 1867 to 1869. In those years (see Table 2) she called at least fifty-seven times, and sometimes

1   Plymouth Custom House (Ply.CH) Register of Ships, Book 2.

2   The *Good Intent* was in fact owned by Messrs Gill and Rundle in 1819. This information was kindly supplied by Grahame Farr.

3   Ply.CH Register of Ships, Book 2. All five barges are registered in this book.

Table 2

Number of occasions on which the barge *Tavistock*
brought lime to Morwellham for the Tavistock Canal, 1867-9

	1867	1868	1869
January	NR	1	O
February	NR	O	2
March	NR	1	1
April	5	4	2
May	4	3	NR
June	7	2	NR
July	1	O	NR
August	3	O	NR
September	3	3	NR
October	3	3	NR
November	4	3	NR
December	O	2	NR

NR - no record

she called at intervals of only two or three days, but never more than seven
times in any one month. In fact none of the barges appear to have gone to
Morwellham more than seven times in a month. The next most regular caller
was the *Edward and Sarah*, built at Calstock by Edward Brooming.[1] She called
on forty-nine occasions, and was closely followed by the *Thomasine*, which
called forty-four times. Other fairly regular callers were the *Albert*,
twenty-six visits, the *John and Ann*, twelve visits, and the *John and Richard*,
ten visits. The number of vessels calling per month between 1867 and 1869,
for the months for which we have records, varied from none to twenty-two.

Although the limestone trade was important and established before the
copper trade, it was this latter trade which was responsible for Morwellham's
great prosperity in the mid-nineteenth century. Unfortunately precise
evidence on the extent of the copper trade, and the complementary commerce
in coal, is sparse, and similarly there is little information on the vessels
in these trades. The normal practice was for a vessel to bring to Morwellham
a cargo of coal from South Wales and then take a return cargo of copper ore
to Swansea. This was not invariably the case, some vessels bringing in coal
but taking out no cargo. Other vessels brought in cargoes other than coal,
the *Batten Castle*, for example, on one occasion brought iron and took out a
cargo of copper. Such movements were probably the exception, and there is
ample evidence from newspapers[2] and harbour reports that many vessels were

1   Details of ownership, sales and place of building of all the barges
    come from the various Plymouth Registers of Shipping.

2   Shipping reports in the Plymouth newspaper, the *Western Daily Mercury*.
    For a general account of the *Batten Castle*, see the paper by Richard
    Pearse also in this volume.

mainly engaged in the coal and copper trades, but unfortunately these reports lack specific references to Morwellham.

As far as coasting vessels were concerned, Morwellham was in an inconvenient position, being so far up the Tamar. For a vessel to reach the quay a pilot was necessary,[1] unless the master was very familiar with the river. For the larger vessels, it was essential that the tide was right, otherwise the vessel would not be able to reach the quay, and then extra days would be added to the passage time. A tow was usually required, too. Similarly on the return journey a pilot and tow were usually necessary, and again the tide had to be suitable. Thus going up to Morwellham was a lengthy business, and most of the vessels engaged in the coal and copper trades took a month to six weeks to make the round trip to and from South Wales. There were exceptions, of course, the *Caroline Phillips* on one occasion taking only twelve days to make the voyage from Morwellham to Swansea.[2]

The first mention of the quay's coal and copper trade and the vessels employed in these trades does not come until the 1830s. In 1836 the Calstock Coastwaiter, who had been recently appointed, came into conflict with the master of a collier, the *Villiers*, when she was at Morwellham.[3] The *Villiers* had come from Swansea, via St Ives with a cargo of coal, which was promptly discharged on the vessel's arrival. Her master then proceeded to take on a cargo of copper ore without having completed the necessary paperwork. The Coastwaiter, besides mentioning this discrepancy, also noted that the *Villiers* traded regularly to Morwellham. The local Plymouth newspapers confirm that she was a regular caller at Plymouth as far back as 1814, but do not give her final destinations.[4]

So far no other evidence has come to light on the vessels involved in both the coal and copper trades of Morwellham. But there are documents which throw light on one or the other trade. For that in coal the Tavistock Canal dues returns are informative for certain years on the numbers and names of the vessels involved.[5] As with the limestone trade the dues rarely show details of vessels and cargoes, but for 1867-9 the records are fuller and some details have also survived for 1864 and 1865. In the year for which records are complete, 1868, coal was brought to Morwellham for the Tavistock Canal on twenty-five occasions (see Table 3).

1   Details for towing and pilots come from the *Batten Castle's* account book and were kindly supplied by Richard Pearse.

2   *Cornwall County Record Office* (CRO) Merchant Shipping Returns, *Caroline Phillips*, Padstow 29358.

3   London Custom House (Ldn.CH) Customs 66/39.

4   See *Plymouth and Dock Telegraph*, 27 August 1814.

5   DRO L1258, Canals, Tavistock Nos. 26, 27, 28 and 29.

Table 3

Number of vessels bringing coal to Morwellham

for the Tavistock Canal, 1864-9

	1864	1865	1867	1868	1869
January	NR	NR	NR	2	O
February	NR	NR	NR	2	O
March	NR	NR	NR	O	1
April	NR	NR	O	1	2
May	NR	NR	1	4	4
June	NR	NR	3	2	3
July	NR	1	3	8	4
August	NR	O	2	4	4
September	NR	2	5	2	3
October	2	NR	1	O	NR
November	O	NR	O	O	NR
December	2	NR	3	O	NR

NR - no record

The imports totalled 3420 tons, which although rather a small quantity, was the usual amount transported along the canal at this time. The Duke of Bedford's accounts certainly show that more coal than this was imported and so other vessels must have brought coal. Unfortunately, the accounts only record when the dues were paid and not when the coal was imported, nor do they always indicate what proportion of the total tonnage was for the Tavistock Canal. It would appear, however, that between two and five times the amount of coal imported for the canal in 1868 was shipped up to Morwellham. It would appear that vessels engaged in the coal and copper trades, individually, brought in a larger tonnage of coal than they took out of copper ore. Thus, for the same tonnage, more vessels were required for shipping out copper than for importing coal. Regarding the frequency with which coal was brought for the Tavistock Canal, Table 3 shows this varied from no cargoes to eight per month, but usually four or less.

Other evidence for the coal or copper trades is sparse. The *Tavistock Gazette* did report the presence of vessels at Morwellham but only if some sombre occurrence was associated with the vessel's stay. Thus in October 1859 the *Providence* of Padstow was recorded as discharging Liverpool coals at Morwellham because a seaman, James Pomery, aged twenty-four, was 'found drowned' in the copper ore dock where the vessel had moved after discharging the coals.[1] In January 1862 the *Speculation* was noted at the quay, three of her crew being charged with stealing coals from Gill and Company.[2]

1   *Tavistock Gazette*, 7 October 1859.

2   *Tavistock Gazette*, 10 January 1862.

In August 1868 the Tavistock Petty Sessions recorded a dispute between the *Eling* and the *Maid of Judah* at Morwellham,[1] this being one of the occasions on which the *Eling* brought coals for the Tavistock Canal. And in July of the same year another accident attested the presence of the *Elizabeth* of Gloucester at the quay, when one of her sailors, named Bell and aged twenty, was drowned.[2]

Morwellham's copper trade also figures in two surviving bills of lading of August 1873.[3] These were both for cargoes of copper ore for the Govenor and Company's CWM Avon Works. Thus the *Mary Hannah* shipped 156 tons of copper ore from Morwellham, and the *Mayflower* 164 tons. The freight rate charged per twenty-one hundred weight was three shillings and six pence. Whether or not the size of cargo was typical will be considered shortly. Another vessel involved in the copper trade was the *Batten Castle*. According to her account book she took copper ore from Morwellham on five occasions between 1852 and 1860. The cargoes ranged in size from 74 to 94 tons, and the usual freight rate, three shillings and six pence.[4]

Some evidence on the Welsh coal trade to Morwellham can be found in the Neath Harbour Records. These show that coal was still being shipped to Morwellham in the latter years of the century: in July 1889 246 tons on the *Tregea*, in October 1889 130 tons on the *Emma Marie*, in March 1895 245 tons on the *Flower of Ake*, and in October 1898 205 tons on the *Lynx*.[5]

With regard to the other, less important, trades of Morwellham, no records relating to lead or tin shipments survive, and there is only one surviving reference each to shipments of manganese and arsenic. In 1868 the *Amphitrite* took a cargo of manganese from Morwellham to Liverpool, and since it was feared that the vessel had been lost on the return voyage her safe arrival back at Plymouth was noted in the *Tavistock Gazette*.[6] And in 1881 a cargo of arsenic was being loaded on to the schooner *Annie* at Morwellham, when an accident occurred to one of her loaders, Richard Simmons, a Morwellham man.[7]

1   *Tavistock Gazette*, 7 August 1868.

2   *Tavistock Gazette*, 24 July 1868.

3   Glamorgan County Record Office (GRO) D/D xnf, 10/4 and 10/7.

4   Information kindly supplied by Richard Pearse.

5   GRO Neath Harbour Records.

6   *Tavistock Gazette*, 26 February 1869.

7   *Western Daily Mercury*, 13 August 1881.

As for the import of iron, the only reference to it in connection with a vessel is in the previously mentioned account book of the *Batten Castle*. This vessel brought pig on four occasions, twice in 1852 and twice in 1854, the size of cargo ranging from 84 to 98 tons. It is certain that other vessels were engaged in this trade in these years. In 1854, for instance, when the *Batten Castle* brought in a total of 184 tons altogether, a total import of 1200 tons is shown in the Bedford accounts.

Concerning timber imports these included both foreign and home-grown supplies. Timber was brought up the Tamar by barge in the early years of the century, and later was floated up in rafts. All foreign, and therefore dutiable, timber had to be unloaded under the super-vision of Customs officials and then kept in a bonded yard. Messrs Gill and Rundle did obtain permission in 1836 for foreign timber to be shipped directly to Morwellham. But they never seem to have made use of this facility, except possibly in 1842, when they requested permission for the bark *Cosmopolite* to land a cargo of British colonial timber at the quay.[1] Permission was granted, but it is doubtful whether she ever went up to Morwellham as she was 373 tons register.

IV

From the admittedly rather sparse evidence presented above, it is possible to make some estimates of the extent of the shipping at Morwellham for at least part of the nineteenth century. Fortunately for the years 1855 to 1865 the Bedford accounts do give some indication of the quantity of goods, in particular copper ore, passing through the quay. Employing these accounts and the available figures of cargo size it is possible to make some rough estimates of the number of vessels required to ship out the copper ore and to bring in the coal and lime-stone. The amounts of copper ore shipped out by vessels from Morwellham, for which we have evidence, range from 74 to 219 tons. The Neath Harbour Records relating to copper ore shipped from quays similar to Morwellham, show that the typical cargo generally ranged from 100 to 150 tons. If the upper figure of 150 tons is taken, then at least 200 vessels must have gone up to Morwellham each year to collect copper in the peak years of 1855 to 1865, and over one hundred vessels when Devon Great Consols started production from 1845. These figures are impressive, especially when one considers that other vessels would have been calling at the quay, bringing coal, iron, etc., and not taking a return cargo of copper. Also there would have been vessels taking on manganese or arsenic, but no copper. Such figures for the number of vessels calling at Morwellham obtain some confirmation from a Custom House, Collector to Board, letter of 1865: 'At the Creek of Calstock there is a decrease of 178 vessels inwards with cargoes as compared with last year, occasioned by their discharge at Plymouth and forwarding the goods by railway to Tavistock'.[2]

1   Ldn.CH Customs 66/44 and 66/165; Ply. CH Register of Ships, Book 4.

2   Ldn.CH Customs 66/61.

Certainly not all those vessels would have been going to Morwellham, but the majority no doubt did.

In 1868, when the quay's trade was already declining, 149 vessels are known to have called at Morwellham, all but three of them for the Tavistock Canal. Of these 146 vessels for the canal, 121 barges brought limestone, and twenty-five coasting vessels brought coal. Reference to the Bedford accounts shows that the Tavistock Canal's imports were just over half the total imports of limestone and coal at this time. It would therefore seem likely that, taking into consideration the vessels carrying goods other than coal, copper and limestone and those which took copper or coal cargoes, but not both, something of the order of 300 vessels called at Morwellham in 1868. And, again, by this year the quay's trade was already on the decline. So that in the peak years of the quay's activity more vessels than this would have called in. Now, as deduced earlier, it would seem that at least 200 vessels a year would have been required to transport Morwellham's copper ore shipments at their peak. And at least 200 barges would have been required to bring in the limestone. Add to that the vessels carrying pig iron, manure, lead, manganese, arsenic, and the other items and the number of vessels at Morwellham would be increased still further. It may well be that in the peak years of activity some 500 vessels annually called at Morwellham quay.[1]

1   On the census night of 1861 (at the beginning of April) ten vessels
    were recorded as being at the quay, and on the similar night a
    decade later, five. DRO RG9 1457, RG10 2146.

APPENDIX

Details of some of the vessels which called at Morwellham in the nineteenth century are given below. Only those vessels for which a reasonable amount of information survives are included.

ALBERT: one of the barges taking limestone to Morwellham. She was built at Calstock in 1863, was of 26 tons and had Calstock owners. Dismantled in 1910.

AMPHITRITE: a schooner of 72 tons, she was built at Padstow in 1859, and had mainly Calstock owners. Her register was transferred to Preston in 1872.

CAMALAN: a schooner of 85 tons, she was built at Padstow in 1849, and was much involved in the coal, culm and copper ore trades. Broken up in 1885.

CAROLINE PHILLIPS: a cutter of 64 tons and built at Padstow in 1862. A fairly regular coal and copper ore trader.

CILICIA: a schooner of 90 tons and built at Padstow in 1860. She was regularly involved in the coal and copper ore trades. Went missing 1875-6.

EDWARD AND SARAH: one of the barges taking limestone to Morwellham, and built by Edward Brooming at Calstock in 1844. She was locally owned until her sinking in 1926.

ELING: one of the vessels bringing coal for the Tavistock Canal. She was built at Eling in 1852, a ketch of 87 tons. She was registered at Bude in 1867, and survived to at least 1870.

ELIZABETH DREW: the last recorded vessel to take a cargo of copper ore from Morwellham. She was built at Padstow in 1871, a schooner of 110 tons, and owned by members of the Sims family. They were merchants in the Tavistock and Gunnislake areas, and ran the manganese mill at Morwellham. An auxiliary engine was added in 1919. She became a total loss in 1933.

FAYAWAY: a schooner of 84 tons and built at Padstow in 1853. She was a regular coal and copper ore trader. She became a total wreck in 1884.

JESSIE BENNETT: one of the last vessels to take copper ore from Morwellham. She was built at Perth in 1868, a brigantine of 135 tons, and was
probably registered there until 1898 when she appears to have been transferred to Fowey. Sunk in a collision in 1902.

JOHN AND ANN: brought limestone to Morwellham for the Tavistock Canal on
a number of occasions. Built at Torpoint in 1833, she was a barge of 26
tons. Dismantled in 1912.

JOHN AND RICHARD: delivered limestone to Morwellham on a number of
occasions. Built at Saltash in 1815, she was a barge of 22 tons.

MAID OF JUDAH: a brigantine of 100 tons, and built at Richibuctu, New
Brunswick, Canada in 1858. In 1859 she was registered at Plymouth and
had Calstock and Gunnislake owners. Went missing in 1874.

REBECCA LANG: a schooner of 72 tons, she was built at Padstow in 1852.
Regularly employed in the South Wales coal and copper ore trade. Lost in
the river Guadalquivir, Spain, December 1868.

RIVAL: of particular interest because she was one of the two vessels owned
by the Morwellham Shipping Company. A schooner of 106 tons and built at
Runcorn in 1862, she was registered at Plymouth in 1864, and was a regular
trader in coal and copper ore. Sank in Holyhead harbour in 1912.

STEPHEN KNIGHT: a schooner of 88 tons, she was built at Bristol in 1813
and registered at Plymouth in 1829. She was mainly employed in the coal
and copper ore trade, until wrecked at St Ives in 1867.

TAMAR QUEEN: a schooner of 103 tons, she was built at Netstakes, Gunnislake,
and mainly Calstock and Gunnislake owned. She traded regularly in the South
Wales coal trade. In 1895 her registry was transferred to Cork.

TAVISTOCK: one of the barges which regularly brought limestone to Morwellham. Of 68 tons she was built at Plymouth in 1794. She was one of the
barges owned by Messrs Gill and Rundle, and survived until about 1889.

WILLIAM AND THOMAS: one of the barges which took limestone to Morwellham.
Of 26 tons, she was built at Saltash in 1831. Foundered near Berry Head in
1909.

Sources:

Board of Trade Shipping Returns
Bedford Tavistock Estate Papers
Lloyd's Register of Shipping
Neath Harbour Records
Plymouth Registers of Shipping
Tavistock Gazette
Western Daily Mercury

Information kindly provided by Mr D B Clement, Mr G Farr, Mr I D Merry and Mr R Pearse

BIBLIOGRAPHY

In addition to the sources cited in the footnotes the following works are informative on Morwellham's trade and shipping in the nineteenth century and earlier.

Frank Booker   *The industrial archaeology of the Tamar valley*
                      (Newton Abbot : David & Charles, 1971)

Herbert P R Finberg   *Tavistock Abbey* (Newton Abbot : David &
                      Charles, 1969)

Basil Greenhill   *The merchant schooners*, Vols 1 & 2 (Newton
                      Abbot : David & Charles, 1968)

William J Slade and   *West Country coasting ketches* (Greenwich :
Basil Greenhill   Conway Maritime Press, 1974)

ACKNOWLEDGEMENTS

I should like to acknowledge the help received in the preparation of this paper. Particular debts are owed to the Trustees of the Bedford Estates for permission to use the Tavistock Estate Papers, and to the Commissioners of Customs for permission to consult documents at the London, Bridgwater, Bristol and Plymouth Custom Houses. I am grateful too to the Cornwall County Record Office, the Devon County Record Office, the Glamorgan County Record Office, and the Plymouth Library for their advice and assistance, and to the Librarian of Lloyd's of London for his aid. Thanks are due also to the Morwellham Open Air Museum for kindly permitting the reproduction of photographs in their keeping.

The *Bessie Belle* and the *Matilda* in the Devon Consols Dock, Morwellham, c.1900

A Tamar barge being towed from her mast, mid-1890s

NAVIGATION SCHOOL AND TRAINING SHIP: EDUCATIONAL PROVISION IN PLYMOUTH

FOR THE MERCANTILE MARINE IN THE NINETEENTH CENTURY

Alston Kennerley

In 1917 A N Whitehead wrote '... education should turn out the pupil with something he knows well and something he can do well'.[1] Although he was writing in the context of a national system of technical education, this statement can usefully be taken to indicate the aims of the particular occupational education which is the subject of this paper, and while it must be recognised that in the popular mind there is a tendency to consider technical education as being synonymous with occupational education, it is necessary to point out that this is not always the case. A technical education in, for example, engineering can be the basis for employment in several different occupations each having a separate programme of occupational education which will be qualified by a number of factors which may not be present in a less specific form of education.

The factors with respect to seafaring may be indicated by the following questions: where does the educational process take place, for what stages in a person's career is it designed, at what level in the occupation is it aimed, what parts of it take place in a formal learning situation, to what extent is it educational in the broad sense, to what extent is it training in the narrow sense?

In craft-based occupations such as seafaring, the 'practical' aspects were learned in an informal learning situation which the master/apprentice relationship was designed to cater for, and which could adapt to changing circumstances unless constrained to a code of rules. Before the middle of the nineteenth century few seafarers could have encountered a formal educational situation. The 'practical' aspects, grouped loosely under the head 'seamanship', were learned on board ship, as could be the rudiments of 'practical navigation', the educational limit of many so-called master mariners. Those who sought a more thorough education in navigation, or whose parents desired it before their sons embarked on a sea career, found it ashore with private teachers of navigation, in the charitable mathematical and navigation schools such as Christ's Hospital or Trinity House School, Hull, or by attending public lectures.[2]

1   Alfred N Whitehead, 'Technical education and its relation to science and literature', in *The aims of education and other essays* (Williams & Norgate, 1929, reprinted, Benn, 1962) p. 74.

2   See David W Waters, *The art of navigation in England in Elizabethan and early Stuart times* (Hollis & Carter, 1958) and Eva G R Taylor, *The mathematical practitioners of Hanoverian England, 1714-1840* (Cambridge UP, 1966).

It is important that the distinction between navigation and
seamanship be understood, because, as shall be seen, many of the shore-
based schools for seafarers were originally established primarily to
teach navigation, and were known by that name. Navigation is the art
of conducting a vessel from one part of the world to another; a route
is chosen taking account of known seabed dangers and likely meteoro-
logical conditions, and the ship's progress is monitored using plane
trigonometry when in sight of land and nautical astronomy when not.
Navigation is the exclusive province of the ship's master and his
officers (or mates). Seamanship embraces all the day-to-day activities
which are involved in running the ship as a propulsion unit, in
maintaining the ship and in the care of its cargo. Some of the duties,
such as handling sail, steering, repairing the rigging, would be
carried out by the seamen (able seamen, ordinary seamen, and boys,
whose foreman is the boatswain), while other duties such as deciding
when to take in sail or altering course to avoid a collision would only
be undertaken by the master or his officers. At times the difference
between navigation and seamanship can become blurred. The actual
taking of a sounding is an aspect of seamanship and would be carried
out by a seaman. The alteration of course to take the ship clear of
shallow water is an act of seamanship undertaken by the master or his
officers, but the alteration of course on the information obtained from
a sounding where no such danger exists, in order to follow a new route,
is an act of navigation.

Seamanship only became a school subject towards the end of the
nineteenth century, when the sailing vessel was giving way to the
power-driven vessel and the prospective officer no longer found it easy
to obtain practical experience at sea in the handling of sail, a facet
of his education which was still a significant part of the examinations
which were established by the Mercantile Marine Act of 1850[1] and which
required ship's masters and their officers to hold Certificates of
Competency. This is exemplified by comparing the equipment inventories
made at the foundation of two navigation schools. That of the Marine
School of South Shields, opened in 1861, expressly for the post-
experience seafarer, lists no items which relate to seamanship although
those relating to navigation, such as compasses, a chronometer, sextants,
globes, are plentiful;[2] that of the Nautical College, Liverpool, opened
in 1892, includes items such as marline spikes, rigging screws, blocks,
sewing palms, in addition to equipment relating to navigation.[3]

After the middle of the nineteenth century a somewhat more organised
approach to nautical education was beginning to appear, and, in addition
to philanthropic and private activity, the beginnings of state
involvement can be seen. A number of factors influenced this development.

1   13 & 14 Vic c. 93.

2   Records held at the Marine and Technical College, South Shields.

3   Proceedings of Liverpool City Council, 1891-2, p. 1306.

In the country as a whole there was the growth of interest in education generally which gave rise to many government educational measures and which also manifested itself in the growing numbers of private and charitable schools. At the same time technical education was developing through the spread of mechanics' institutes and later the civic colleges.

As well as such general influences the growth of educational provision for seafarers can be attributed to more particular factors. The perennial concern over the supply of seamen for the Royal Navy in time of war, almost a national phobia, continued throughout the century. The strength of this concern may be judged from the fact that, in a petition from the Borough of Plymouth, dated 6 July 1803, against a bill for 'Creating a company for the more effectually supplying the Metropolis with fish ...', a major argument read:

> That the advantages arising from the British Fisheries to the nation in providing a nursery for seamen for the Royal Navy are so obvious as to need no observations from your petitioners and they conceive that the bill now under consideration will materially prevent any increase in the numbers of fishing vessels ...[1]

Again in 1810 we find the Mayor of Plymouth calling a meeting to consider a bill 'to increase the number of persons to be bred to the sea service',[2] while a later example is found in the Royal Commission on Manning the Navy, 1858-59, which was appointed:

> to enquire into the best means of manning the navy, and into what manner and under what arrangements seamen may be readily obtained for such purpose during peace, or in case of sudden emergency or war ...[3]

Another factor which influenced the growth of nautical education was the public realisation of the scandalously inadequate educational level of many mercantile marine officers, which was put on record by the Select Committee of Shipwrecks, 1836, whose report recommended, amongst other things, the institution of examinations for mercantile marine officers and the establishment of nautical schools.[4] The former recommendation was eventually effected by the 1850 Act[5] while a start with the latter was made by the Marine Department of the Board of Trade with schools in London and Liverpool in 1853 and 1854. From 1856[6] the scheme for cheap nautical

---

1   Devon Record Office (DRO) W 668 T.

2   DRO W 668 T.

3   *British Parliamentary Papers (BPP)* 1859, VI, 1.

4   *BPP*, 1836, XVII.

5   13 & 14 Vic c.93.

6   First report of the Department of Science and Art, *BPP*, 1854, XXXI, 299.

schools was managed and extended by the Department of Science and Art.[1]

There was a distinct difference between the establishments engendered by these concerns: the problem of the supply of seamen gave rise to schools (and training ships) for the 'pre-sea' education of boy seamen (that is an education with a nautical bias for boys who were expected to go to sea); the schools which were developed during the 1850s were principally involved in 'post-experience' education, though there were also developments in pre-sea education for intending officers. The two Plymouth-based establishments, the Training Ship *Mount Edgcumbe* and the Plymouth School of Navigation, are representatives of these two types.

II

On 24 October 1862 the *Western Morning News* reported to its readers: We understand that the Plymouth Local Marine Boards have at last decided to establish a Nautical School in connection with the Mercantile Marine Department of the Board of Trade, under the superintendence of a duly qualified and certificated master, at which the highest amount of nautical instruction will be given at the lowest possible cost.

The Plymouth School of Navigation appears to have been the first school in Devon and Cornwall to offer subsidised instruction to seafarers, if one excludes teachers such as Thomas Drake who was licensed, on 4 February 1754, to teach reading, writing, arithmetic and navigation[2] at the charity school, Gittisham, but it was not the first time such an idea had been placed before the citizens of Plymouth. In 1815 a group of 'the most respectable of merchants' had established a Marine School in Liverpool and the following year sent a copy of their annual report to 'every considerable seaport of the United Kingdom' urging 'the establishment of similar institutions...'[3]

It must not be assumed that the new school at Plymouth filled a vacuum; almost every port could boast a private navigation teacher (the larger ones had several) and a new school would have to prove itself in what was, after 1850, inevitably its main work: helping seafarers to pass the Board of Trade's examinations. It probably, however, filled a need in that, because its fees were low compared with private schools, nautical education was brought within the reach of a group of seafarers who might not have been able to afford it. In a field where a successful pass rate would attract students it is not surprising to find that some sponsored schools led uneasy existences. At Leith,

---

1   For a more detailed study see, Clifford Jeans,'The first statutory qualifications for seafarers', *Transport History*, VI, 1973, 248-67.

2   DRO Exeter Diocesan Registers of Licences and Perpetual Cures.

3   DRO W 668 T.

following the departure of its first head to Glasgow, the school ran down rapidly and was for a time closed down.[1] At South Shields the Marine School suffered for many years from severe competition from local private schools.[2] In Devon and Cornwall private navigation teachers are recorded, at various dates, in Torpoint, Teignmouth, Bideford, Dartmouth, the Scillies and Exeter, while in the three towns of Plymouth, Stonehouse and Devonport at least four schools or teachers existed in 1852.[3] After 1883, however, only references to the School of Navigation have been found.

The sponsored navigation schools were not established without considerable care by the authorities to ensure that there was suitable local management, that the finance provided was used effectively and that the teachers selected were the best that could be found. During the early years of the Department of Science and Art, before attention to the Navigation Schools was swamped by the growing mass of its work in other areas, deliberate efforts were made to encourage the establishment of schools in the leading ports and so influence the nature of the education made available that the schools provided a broadly based syllabus for all levels of seafaring, especially pre-sea. In order to provide a body of suitably trained and certificated teachers for the new schools a training programme was inaugurated whereby pupil teachers from the Royal Naval School at Greenwich were sent to the London Science and Art Navigation School to attend scientific courses.[4]

No local records relating to the Plymouth School in the last century have been located, but some idea of the method adopted for the establishment of the schools may be obtained from that at Leith. The Provost called a meeting of interested parties: the Senior Bailie, the Master and Assistant Master of Trinity House, the Chairman of the Chamber of Commerce, two members of the Seamen's Friend Society and two of the Local Marine Board. Dr Lyon Playfair represented the Board of Trade and outlined the conditions under which the Board would co-operate with the local authorities in the establishment and maintenance of a nautical school. The local committee was to comprise the nine local persons attending the meeting, the master's salary would be guaranteed and a grant made for apparatus, if the committee provided the accommodation and funds for its furnishing. Of the fees collected from students half was to be devoted to the maintenance of the school and half to go to the teacher as his salary. Advice was provided by Mr Hughes, head of the Royal Naval School at Greenwich,

1   Leith Nautical College records.

2   Information supplied by staff of South Shields Marine and Technical College.

3   Devon, Cornwall and Plymouth directories.

4   *BPP*, 1854, XXXI, 299.

and the Department of Science and Art recommended the first Master, John Newton.[1] In Plymouth only the names of the first chairman, Thomas Restarick and secretary, William Bennett Cumming are known,[2] but as the school is at times referred to as the 'Marine Board Navigation School' it is likely that its committee of management was the Local Marine Board or comprised the same persons. Certainly Cumming, 'a surveyor of shipping' was a member of the Board in 1881[3] and had previously examined for Trinity House in Plymouth during the period of voluntary examinations (1845-50).[4]

The *Western Daily Mercury*[5] recorded what was probably the first inspection, and might have been the official opening of the 'Plymouth New Navigation *Schools*' by its managers, '... the *Schools* having been properly furnished and prepared for use' (author's italics). One might infer from the use of the plural that a major establishment of some considerable size had been set up, but this was not the case; there were simply different classes for the various levels of instruction. The return of the School to the Department of Science and Art reveals:

> ... the total number of students receiving instruction in or
> through the agency of the School during 1863 has been 240
> [and] the entire number of adults and boys who have at any
> time paid fees during the year are: masters 39, chief mates
> 26, only mates 70, second mates 39, master home trade 1,
> mate home trade 1, second engineer 1, seamen 10, apprentices
> 6, boys 22. The number of boys who have gone to sea during
> the year is 18 ... most of the students attend both day and
> evening classes.

According to the *Mercury* 'the charges to be paid for nautical instructions by the different grades of officers, men and boys were to vary from 6d. to 6/- per week'. These fees may be compared with those of the Torpoint Naval School in which Mr Hall, Master R.N., F.R.G.S., offered 'advanced instruction in practical navigation, marine surveying and the use of nautical instruments' to 'naval cadets, master's assistants, masters and mates of the mercantile marine' for one guinea per month in advance.[6] The subsidy at the Navigation School assisted seamen at the start of their careers or when studying for their first qualifications while those well established and presumably better able to bear it paid the full fees. This was in line with the general policy of the Department of trying to improve the education of the next generation of seafarers.

1   Leith Nautical College records.

2   10th report of Department of Science and Art, *BPP,* 1863, XVI, 21.

3   *Plymouth Directory,* 1880-1.

4   *Plymouth, Devonport and Stonehouse Herald,* 24 March 1849, p.8; also *BPP,* 1847, LX, 526-7.

5   3 January 1863, p.5.

6   *Western Morning News,* 17 January 1863, p.8, advertisement.

It is difficult to say how many students were present at any one time, but during 1863, assuming a school year of 40 weeks, the average number of boys present at any one time was seven while the average period of attendance by boys was sixteen weeks, if the boys paid at the lowest rate. It is interesting to note that when the Liverpool Nautical College was established in 1892, James Gill, its first head, organised it into four schools : for Boys, Apprentices and Seamen, Candidates for the Board of Trade Certificates and Officers.[1]

As already indicated, the Department of Science and Art's financial aid for apparatus took the form of matching the funds provided from local sources. When the Leith School was opened (1855) '£100 was allowed in aid of outfit if the local committee would spend an equal amount'. Hull and Sunderland (1855) were to be supplied with the necessary apparatus at half cost, while in 1859 the grant of £105 to the Sunderland school towards the expenses of building is described as exceptional. The arrangements for supporting teachers' salaries were more complicated and were varied from time to time. In 1855 Mr Bolt, the master at Sunderland, was to retain half the fee, the allowance for his certificate was to be £10, while he was guaranteed £100 for the first year. The following year the maximum certificate allowance was set at £50. In 1860 it was ruled that a certificated master could earn certificate allowances firstly of £6, £4 or £2 (dependent on the grade of his certificate) for each boy taught by him who was apprenticed on a merchant vessel, and secondly £1 for each seaman, mate or master who, having received at least 20 lessons from him, passed an examination at the local Marine Board for Higher Certificates.[2]

The buildings which first housed these navigation schools were diverse in many respects, but they did appear to have one thing in common: they were located within easy access of the seafarer. Leith's first accommodation was in the Mariner's Church only across Commercial Road from the docks. In London and Liverpool rooms were taken in the Sailors' Homes. In Plymouth the School's first home was in an adapted private house, 13½ Gascoyne Place, not exactly in dockland but only 15 minutes walk from Sutton Harbour and close to Friary Station.

This then is the context into which John Merrifield, the Plymouth School of Navigation's first head, moved when he left Mary Tavy National School in the summer of 1862. Did he meet the standards set by the Department of Science and Art? He had trained at the Exeter Diocesan Training College and had obtained good results, especially in scientific subjects. The reports of the inspectors during the long probationary period were good and he now held the Board of Education's Teacher's Certificate.[3] In 1861 he had obtained the Department of Science and Art

1   Liverpool Council Proceedings, 1891-2.

2   Department of Science and Art Minutes on Navigation Schools.

3   Plymouth Central Library, Merrifield's certificate - reproduced at
     the end of this paper.

Teacher's Certificate in chemistry and in 1862 obtained a first class
in steam. His studies continued after taking on his new appointment
and by 1865 he held certificates in mathematics, chemistry, navigation,
nautical astronomy, steam stability and physical geography. In 1867 he
was awarded the Gold Medal for applied mechanics and the Bronze for
theoretical mechanics, and in 1868 the Gold Medal for magnetism and
electricity, the Bronze for navigation and the Gold for nautical
astronomy.[1] Like the masters appointed to lead the other navigation
schools Merrifield was young, had studied a wide range of subjects, and,
unlike many of the private teachers, he was not a seafarer.

It has not been possible to build up a clear picture of the year
by year fortunes of the School by using the returns published in the
Science and Art Directories. Until 1871, when 192 admissions are
recorded, the figures are almost certainly the totals of all enrolments,
and one can conclude that the school had no difficulty in attracting
students, a peak of 379 admissions being achieved only two years after
its opening. But in 1872 only 8 admissions are recorded, and thereafter
a much lower number obtains. In the 1890s these figures are labelled
'evening'. This change can probably be attributed to a tightening up by
the Department in the nature of the returns so that only those students
genuinely studying for Science and Art qualifications could be included.

In 1863, in an attempt to bring the Navigation Schools into line
with other Science and Art classes, the Department cancelled all its
previous minutes on Navigation Schools and imposed the following
conditions for gaining its financial support.[2]

- Aid would be granted only on the results of teaching in the five
  subjects of navigation, nautical astronomy, mathematics, physical
  geography and steam.

- Payments would only be made to certificated teachers.

- Teacher's examinations would be held in London, Edinburgh and
  Dublin in November.

- Student's examinations would be held: for adults four times a
  year at the seaports by the Local Marine Boards; for boys once
  a year as part of the general May examination.

- The grades of success would be pass, honourable mention, third,
  second and first grade certificates.

- The teacher's related results payments would be £1, £2, £3, £4
  or £5 : for a boy if 40 lessons had been taken and he went to sea;
  for adults if 20 lessons had been taken.

1   Science and Art Directories.

2   Science and Art Minute R87, 15 April 1863.

- The lessons must have been taken since the last results payment.

- A local committee must be formed.

The regulations were too arduous for the context in which the
schools operated and several appear to have immediately given up the
fight to obtain aid from the Science and Art Department. In 1862 the
directory listed 16 navigation schools. This figure dropped to 11 the
following year, to six in 1871, and in 1876 three remained: Hull Trinity
House (which concentrated on pre-sea education and had long been
considered satisfactory by the Department), Plymouth and Leith.[1] That
Plymouth and Leith continued to receive aid while other schools closed or
joined the ranks of the private schools, may perhaps be attributed to a
relaxation of the rigid attitude to Navigation Schools on the part of the
Department. In 1870 at the suggestion of Leith capitation grants were
introduced, and although they were subject to renewal each year Plymouth
was still in receipt of such a grant in 1900.[2]

It is unlikely that Merrifield could have run the school without the
help of assistants for more than a year, but he alone is listed as
receiving Science and Art payments before 1872 when the name of J.W. White
appears. Charles Morris is first listed in 1874, and W.V. Merrifield,
John Merrifield's son, appears from 1877. Two other Merrifields, S S and
R H , are listed in 1878 and 1879.[3] W V Merrifield was a Cambridge
graduate and may have succeeded his father about 1886 as head;[4] he later,
in the 1890s, took over the headship of Liverpool Nautical College, the
headship at Plymouth passing to Charles Morris. In 1881 E.M. Minhinnick
is first listed, and his name and that of Charles Morris appear in an
advertisement offering evening classes in mathematics, nautical astronomy,
animal physiology and hygiene in 1897.[5]

In order to receive the results payments Merrifield's staff, though
not so well qualified perhaps as himself, must have held the Department
of Science and Art teacher's Certificates and therefore one of the
original aims of the supporters of navigation schools - providing well
educated and qualified teachers - was continued at Plymouth throughout the
century.

It is much less certain that the School was able to fulfil
consistently that early aim of actually giving seafarers a broad education.
Less than five years after the School opened, Capt. Donnelly, the
Department of Science and Art Inspector for Science, giving evidence before

1   Science and Art Directories.

2   Science and Art Minutes, 3 November 1870, 31 December 1870.

3   Science and Art Directories.

4   John Merrifield's obituary, *Western Weekly Mercury*, 4 July 1891.

5   *Western Morning News*, 28 September 1897, p.3.

the Select Committee on Scientific Instruction, said, in answer to a
question about the School, 'it is simply a cramming school for the
Board of Trade Examinations'; and compared it unfavourably with the
Hull School - 'they are very successful there'.[1] This contrasts
with the opinion of the Plymouth Local Marine Board who supported
their request for the appointment of an engineer examiner at
Plymouth with a reference to the Navigation School 'the master of
which is a first class teacher'.[2] But perhaps it helps to explain why
on the title page of his book, *Navigation and Nautical Astronomy,*
which was written in 1868, Merrifield describes himself with the
curious phrase 'of the Science School, and Head Master of the
Navigation School, Plymouth'.[3] Was he already disillusioned about the
ability of the school, in the existing climate, to run real educational
classes for seafarers rather than just 'cramming' classes for the Board
of Trade examinations, given, on the one hand, the almost impossible
conditions in which finance was available from the Department of Science
and Art, and, on the other, seafarers who would be prepared to pay the
economic cost of only the minimum instruction which would get them
through the examination? In addition, one must not forget that,
although in time Merrifield's school came to be the only one in Plymouth,
he was, because of the mobility of seafarers, in effect in competition
with all the other navigation schools in the country.

John Merrifield died in 1891, aged 56 years, and the scale of his
reputation can be measured in the size of his obituaries,[4] in which his
achievements as a writer on navigation and magnetism, for which he had
an international reputation, as a meteorologist, as the holder of
honorary degrees, as a prominent member of the Plymouth School Board
and as head of the Navigation School, get full recognition.

III

The Plymouth training ship *Mount Edgcumbe,* like many others run by
voluntary organisations and by the Royal Navy during the nineteenth
century, was not a sea-going vessel. She was moored permanently on the
River Tamar off Saltash just north of the Brunel railway bridge. Such
vessels were often old men-of-war, no longer fit for active service.
The training ship movement perhaps owes its origins to the Marine Society,

1   *BPP,* 1867-8, XV, p.8.

2   Public Record Office (PRO) MT9/22, W948/64.

3   John Merrifield and Henry Ever, *Navigation and nautical astronomy*
     (Longmans, Green, 1873).

4   *Western Weekly Mercury,* 4 July 1891; *Naval and Military Record,*
     2 July 1891, p.13.

formed in 1756 by Jonas Hanway, who 'must be credited with providing more men for the Navy than any other man in history'.[1] It established its training ship *Warspite* in 1783 as a holding base for the boys it was sponsoring while berths in suitable vessels were being sought. But the use of old ships as training bases did not become popular until the middle of the nineteenth century. In 1859 the Royal Commission on Manning the Navy recommended that:

> school ships should be established in the principal commercial ports capable of accommodating 100 to 200 boarders in each ship, of whom 100 should be supported by the state.[2]

And further, that they should be open to day scholars, old boys between voyages, and that boys should get the requisite instruction for the merchant service and for the Royal Navy. The Royal Navy took up the idea and by 1874 its own arrangements were considered to have been very successful.[3] Certainly much of the Royal Navy's training activity was centred on its training ships well into the twentieth century.

For the training ships run by other organisations, finance was always a problem. The Admiralty usually loaned the ships themselves, but conversion and operating expenses had to be met from other sources. Direct finance from the government was not made available, and the only state aid which could be tapped was that available under the Reformatory and Industrial Schools Acts, 1866.[4] Nevertheless between 1856 and 1885 some twenty-one training ships were established. Of these, the *Conway* and *Worcester* were fee-paying and devoted to the education and training of future officers. The remainder attempted to train future seamen. Five relied entirely on voluntary donations for income; three were operated under the Reformatory Schools Act; the remainder under the Industrial Schools Act. Although a few of these ships were founded with the support of sections of the shipping industry, the majority came into existence as the result of local philanthropic effort.

It is not clear who the 'moving spirit' was behind *Mount Edgcumbe*'s establishment, but the inaugural meeting was held in Plymouth on 5 November 1874 (there were parallel meetings in Stonehouse and Devonport).[5] The work of the training ship at Bristol (the *Formidable*) was described. Mr W F Moore, moving the establishment of a ship, revealed that the Admiralty would support the venture and said that 'the prejudice which had previously existed in the minds of many persons not

1   Christopher Lloyd, *The British seaman* (Collins, 1968, reprinted Paladin, 1970) p.171.

2   *BPP*, 1859, VI, xv. For the location of the various civilian training ships established in the nineteenth century, see the map at the end of this paper.

3   Final report of the royal commission on unseaworthy ships, *BPP*, 1874, XXXIV, xiv.

4   29 & 30 Vic c.117 and c.118. These Acts consolidated earlier measures and were themselves subsequently amended.

5   *Western Daily Mercury*, 5 November 1874, p.3.

connected with the mercantile marine' had to be broken down. A committee of thirty-three persons was elected. Thus the Devon and Cornwall Industrial Training Ship Association came into existence.

A year later the Committee reported that £2,000 had been promised in donations for fitting out the ship and £114 in annual subscriptions. In addition the patronage of many of the local aristocracy had been enlisted. The Earl of Devon regarded the matter as one of national importance, while Sir Massey Lopes said the objectives were both philanthropic and patriotic. But Mr W F Collier noted the small attendance of the shipping interest. Mr Sampson Lloyd, M.P., attributed many casualties at sea to imperfect nautical education and noted the small support of the government.[1]

The vessel which was inaugurated as the *Mount Edgcumbe* in June 1877 had started life as H.M.S. *Winchester,* built at Woolwich between 1816 and 1822, to a Seppings design, with round stern, diagonal frames, of the Java class of 60-gun frigates. She was 487 tons ordinary measure and in service had a company of 450 including 70 marines. In 1861 she became the second *Conway,* and was relinquished following an epidemic in 1874 which revealed her defects: bad ventilation in the lower deck, and lack of space for an isolation ward and bathroom.[2] She was refitted at a cost of £2,100 and registered for 250 boys under the Industrial Schools Act.[3] The vessel was fully rigged as a barque and newly coppered and painted. Donations had reached £3,408 of which all but £1,000 had been spent. Annual subscriptions had reached £525, still well below the £580 needed for salaries and £260 for other running costs.[4] By February 1878 150 boys had been admitted and the staff at that time comprised the Captain-Superintendent, Chief Officer, Schoolmaster, three Seamen Instructors, Carpenter and Cook. The acceptance of the Admiralty offer of a Gunnery Officer caused some concern at the quarterly meeting of the Committee as 'many people had subscribed to the idea of a ship for the *Merchant Navy*'.[5]

The financial details given in the newspaper reports require clarification. The *Mount Edgcumbe* Committee might seem to have been fortunate in obtaining a vessel which had already been converted for use as a training ship. However, the amount spent on refitting was

1   *Western Daily Mercury,* 27 November 1875, p.3.

2   John Masefield, *The Conway* (Heinemann, 1933) pp.23, 35.

3   *Western Daily Mercury,* 14 June 1877, p.6.

4   *Western Daily Mercury,* 27 July 1877, p.4.

5   *Western Daily Mercury,* 5 February 1878, p.2.

similar to that spent on fitting out the *Formidable*, which suggests that the *Mount Edgcumbe* needed fairly extensive repairs.[1] The sum of £580 annually for salaries seems very low. If this was to cover the level of staffing indicated in February 1878, then the staff was probably being paid at the lowest annual rates found at any of the other training ships:[2]

	Lowest salary at other training ships	*Formidable*
	£	£
Captain-Superintendent	225	350
Chief Officer	80	120
Schoolmaster	50	175
Seaman Instructor	40	65
Seaman Instructor	40	65
Seaman Instructor	40	65
Carpenter	54	85
Cook	45	65
	£574	£990

Once the full complement of 250 boys was reached it is likely that the number of staff was increased to between 12 and 18, the staffing levels of the *Indefatigable* and the *Southampton*, both accommodating 250 boys. The former received destitute boys and relied entirely on donations for its finance. Its staff included two additional seamen instructors to the eight indicated above for the *Mount Edgcumbe*. The latter was an industrial school ship and its additional staff included one school-master, two seamen instructors, two tailors, a bandmaster, a steward, a shoemaker, and a medical officer. The sum of £260 for other running costs probably applied to office expenses and routine servicing costs to the ship itself, as it could not have covered the expense of feeding and clothing the boys. In 1874 the total annual expenditure of the *Southampton* was £4002 3s 9d of which only £86 4s 11d was received in private donations; the bulk of its income came from the Treasury as grants under the Industrial Schools Act.[3] These grants were paid at the rate of 6s per head per week.

In order to receive state support the management committee of the *Mount Edgcumbe* had to apply to the Home Office for certification as an industrial school. This would be granted as a result of an inspection and a satisfactory report by an inspector of industrial schools. In addition the proposed school rules had to be approved, the school was subject to inspection at least annually, and any proposed changes had to receive approval. Home Office control meant that the various training ships were run in a generally uniform manner, and that suitable records

1   Inspector's report, 11 November 1869, PRO HO45/9898/B18641.

2   Report of the special committee on the cost of the *Shaftesbury* and on the staff, 26 February 1879, appendix 23, PRO HO45/9551/62793.

3   Thomas Brassey, *British seamen* (Longmans, 1877) p.51.

were kept. The *Mount Edgcumbe's* records were lost during the 1939-45 war, but those of several other ships have survived. 'The rules and regulations for the management of the Bristol training ship *Formidable*' required the Captain-Superintendent to keep a register book, a log book or journal, a conduct book, a cash book, a general order book and a visitors' book.[1] A not untypical entry in the register book reads:

> George Oakley, No. 257. Admitted 30.9.1872; aged 12;
> born 9 Nov. 1859. Detained under section 14 till 16 years.
> From Southwark. Cannot read, write or cypher. Protestant.
> 1 week in school. Father sober; 4 sisters, 2 brothers.
> Employed 2 months with father (brass finisher), 10 months
> in a coal shop, 2 years fruit sorting in Convent Garden.
> Conduct on board very good. No punishments. On leaving:
> character very good; educational standard IV; reading,
> writing and cyphering fairly good. Discharged 30 Nov. 1874.
> Apprenticed for 3 years to barque *Callisto* of Sunderland,
> age 15.

Under section 14 of the Industrial Schools Act any person could bring any child under the age of 14 years before a magistrate. If the child was found to be in need of care and protection, he could be committed to a certified industrial school for as long as was considered necessary but not beyond the age of 16 years. The child might be sent to any school on shore (or a training ship) which had space and agreed to accept him. The training ships were probably favoured for the more unruly cases as they were run on naval lines and the discipline was considered to be stricter than that at other schools. Although children under the age of 12 years charged with an imprisonable offence could also be sent to an industrial school, children in such schools had not been convicted. Parents could apply to have their children sent to an industrial school if they were out of control, and the training ships also accepted children on a voluntary basis, the parents paying boarding fees. Between 1869 and 1909 the *Formidable* received 183 volunteers out of a total of 4049 boys admitted. For boys sent to the *Mount Edgcumbe* under the Act the age range was originally 11 to 15 years, later raised to 12 to 16 years. However, on occasion, boys were admitted as young as ten years of age.

From the outset the *Mount Edgcumbe* seems to have received a significant proportion of her intake from other parts of the country, particularly London.[2] In 1896, out of 68 boys admitted, the ship received 51 from London, two each from Plymouth, Stonehouse, Devonport and Exeter, and one each from Barnstaple, Cullompton, Truro, Jersey, Yarmouth, Hereford, Fowey, Cawsand and St. Germains.[3] The ship was not the only industrial school in Devon and Cornwall, and the area was not as heavily populated as other parts of the country. In 1875 the Devon

[1] Whenever reference is made to the *Formidable* in the following paragraphs the data has been abstracted from the ship's registers and annual reports, which are held at T.S. *Formidable*, Portishead, a shore establishment, now a local authority community home.

[2] *Western Daily Mercury*, 5 February 1878, p.2.

[3] *Western Morning News*, 31 August 1897, p.8.

and Exeter Boys Industrial School accommodated 53 boys from Devon and Cornwall.[1] From the comments in newspaper reports at various dates, it seems likely that for the greater part of her existence the *Mount Edgcumbe* operated at below her full complement of 250 boys.

The Ship's responsibility for its boys did not necessarily cease once they were about to be discharged. Some were released on licence if a suitable occupational opening occurred, and these could be recalled if reports were unsatisfactory. All boys were provided with a full outfit of clothing, and an attempt was made to keep track of all 'old boys' for a year or two after discharge through letters from boys, employers' reports and agents' reports. Although the emphasis was on a seafaring training and thus boys were inevitably being influenced to choose that occupation, there was no obligation to do so. Of the boys discharged from the *Mount Edgcumbe* in 1896, 13 went into the merchant service, 4 to the army, 32 to friends, 3 to naval service, 1 to Canada and 3 had died. This may not have been a typical year, however, since all the training ships were experiencing difficulty at that time owing to the increasing proportion of steam shipping, the unwillingness of many owners, particularly steamship owners, to employ boys in any capacity, and the large numbers of foreign seamen being employed on British ships. Between 1869 and 1909 the *Formidable* discharged 2312 boys to the merchant service, 192 to the Royal Navy, 358 to friends, 82 to the army, 67 died, 460 were found other employment, and 229 were discharged for other reasons. Few boys were accepted by the Royal Navy because few could meet its physical standards. The fault did not lie with the ships but with the poor living conditions in which many boys had spent their early childhood. The same reason might also in part account for the deaths which occurred amongst the boys. Their resistance to illness would not be so strong. However, there was concern at the difficulty of maintaining health on training ships, none of which were easy to adapt and maintain; the enclosed environment allowed infection to spread rapidly and epidemics of opthalmia, scarlet fever and typhoid, for example, were experienced.[2]

The functions of industrial schools originally included the idea that, as well as imparting a basic education and the basic skills of a craft occupation, the schools could be partially self-financing through the sale of the product of the pupils' industrial labour. The main industry of the Devon and Exeter Boys Industrial School was agriculture, with tailoring, shoemaking, wireworking and firewood cutting; it is not difficult to envisage surplus agricultural produce being sold locally.

1   *Western Daily Mercury*, 10 October 1875, p.4.

2   Report of a statement by Harry Leach, Medical Officer of Health for London, *The Times*, 11 November 1875, p.11.

But in the case of the industrial training ships the main industry was
seamanship which does not produce saleable goods. The subsidiary
industries of tailoring and shoemaking served only to save on the
purchase of clothing for the boys, and as the ship had to purchase
cloth and leather, and employ a tailor and shoemaker to supervise the
activity, the saving could only have been marginal.

A boy sent to the *Mount Edgcumbe* would have found himself drawn
into a way of life which was almost certainly in marked contrast to his
previous existence. While his personal needs of food, clothing and
housing were provided, the very full daily routine occupied all his
waking hours from about 5.30 in the morning to 8 at night throughout the
year.[1] Of this time about one and a half hours would have been spent at
meals, three hours each at 'household' duties, 'school' and 'seamanship',
etc, and the remainder at recreation and other miscellaneous duties.
The boys were divided into two watches, port and starboard; during the
morning, while one watch was at 'school' the other was at 'seamanship',
during the afternoon the roles were reversed. Each watch was further
divided into a number of divisions and messes. Each division contained
about 30 boys and was supervised by one member of staff aided by two or
three senior boys. The messes were smaller units which functioned at
meal times; each boy in turn would serve food in his mess. There were
numerous other duties which the boys took turns at performing, such as
post boy or messenger. In fact the organisation of the Ship simulated
that of the adult world of Royal Naval ships.

The watch 'on deck' (at seamanship) was divided into various
groups supervised by the seaman-instructors. All the skills of the
practical seaman were taught including knots and splices, canvas work,
sail handling, boat handling, signalling, sounding and compass work.
For safety reasons the 'abandon ship' drill was thoroughly practised and
the *Mount Edgcumbe* was noted for its efficiency. Each boy also spent
time working under the supervision of the cook, the carpenter, the tailor
and the shoemaker. The watch 'below' was meanwhile at school on the main
deck, immediately below the upper deck. Except for sections towards the
bows and stern which had been partitioned off for staff accommodation,
the galley, stores and boys' bathroom, the main deck was a large open
space which served, as occasion required, as dining room, class room,
assembly hall and recreation room. For 'school' the boys were divided
into classes according to their standard at reading, writing and arithmetic, all classes being held together in the same space. On the
Formidable in 1875 half an hour daily was devoted to scripture and three-
quarters of an hour each to reading, writing and arithmetic; top classes
received one lesson in geography and one in history each week, and all
classes received a weekly singing lesson and a weekly 'object' lesson.
The most advanced boys were taught navigation, and some boys were given

---

1   The following paragraphs are based in part on the *Formidable* records.
     The author is also indebted to the following persons for information
     about the *Mount Edgcumbe*: Mrs F Parcelle, daughter of Capt. W H
     Harkcom, last Captain-Superintendent; Mr H F Rawlings, assistant
     schoolmaster on the ship in 1914; Mr Alfred S Smith, who served as a
     boy on board the ship between 1910 and 1912; and Mr Marshall Ware,
     whose father supplied coal to the ship.

additional lessons in the evening. At the end of the school period
the desks were stacked away and replaced by the tables and benches for
the meal which followed. Although the main deck was one large open
space, invisible boundaries 'marked' the area occupied by a particular
activity, and a boy wishing to enter or cross an area was required to
ask permission. At meal times, for example, each mess occupied such a
space. The *Mount Edgcumbe* was equipped with a small library, an organ,
brass band instruments, and a variety of games, and during the evening
the main deck became the scene of a variety of recreational activities.
At the end of the day hammocks were slung in the lower deck, below the
main deck, which served as the dormitory.

Because the *Mount Edgcumbe* was a residential establishment there
had to be a staff presence twenty four hours a day. This was normally
maintained on a rota basis by the Captain-Superintendent, Chief Officer
and the Seamen-Instructors, all of whom had naval backgrounds. Only
the Captain-Superintendent and his family lived on board, in spacious
accommodation at the after end of the ship. The other staff lived
ashore but had their own rooms on board as they kept duty on alternate
nights and alternate weekends. At night, watches of two hours duration
were kept by one member of staff aided by two boys.

Opportunity for boys to leave the ship to spend time ashore was not
very frequent. Saturday afternoons were set aside for games in a field
to which the ship had been given access, but, especially in winter, this
could be prevented by adverse weather, and there were times when the
waters in Saltash Passage were too rough for any of the ship's boats to
be operated. Home leave seems to have been rarely granted, though a few
boys were allowed home at Christmas. There was, however, greater
opportunity for shore leave during the summer months, especially for the
ship's band which was invited to play at local fêtes.

The *Mount Edgcumbe* was able to provide its boys with ample small
boat experience through its fleet of small craft which, in 1898, included
a 7-ton yawl, four cutters and three gigs.[1] However, like the other
training ships of this type, it was unable to provide any sea-going
experience. Several of the training ships overcame this drawback through
the acquisition of a small sea-going sailing vessel as a 'tender'. The
Polly, a brigantine, was attached to the *Formidable* in 1875 and was
included in her certification as an industrial school to ensure that
grants would be received while boys were aboard the tender. That the
Mount Edgcumbe did not acquire such a vessel until 1898, may perhaps be
attributed to her less favourable financial circumstances. Apart from
capital costs, there were additional maintenance expenses to be met and
the salaries of four more members of staff to be found. Her new tender
Goshawk was a brig of 150 tons and accommodated about 30 boys. During
the next few years she cruised in the Channel during the summer months,
being laid up in the Cattewater during the winter.

---

1   Report of the inspection by Capt. Stopford, RN, PRO HO 45/9824/B8262E.

IV

The foregoing discussion has been concerned with the recognition
during the nineteenth century of the need for improvement in the
standard of education and training amongst merchant seafarers, and
with the response in Plymouth which led to the founding of two
establishments, a navigation school and a training ship, both of which
have been examined in some detail with reference to their inception
and operation to about 1900. In this final section an attempt will be
made to evaluate their contribution. A brief outline of the subsequent
history of the two organisations will also be given.

Did the *Mount Edgcumbe* and the Plymouth School of Navigation have
anything in common with each other? In the seafaring context the
former was concerned with the pre-sea education and training of future
seamen, the latter with the post-experience and pre-sea education and
training of future officers. In the educational context the former
was an elementary school which occasionally found itself with a higher
grade pupil, the latter was a school for further education which at
times had to engage in remedial teaching. This might seem to be the
extent of any similarities, and in detail it is perhaps true. But in
general there were several aspects in common. Both came into being in
response to a national need for better qualified seafarers, and each
was a manifestation of a particular national movement: their counter-
parts were to be found in other ports. It should, however, be noted
that both establishments were amongst the last of their type to be
established, and this might possibly be associated with the fact that
Plymouth was much more a naval port than a commercial port. Again,
the Ship and the School were non-profit making and managed by independent
committees which found it convenient to comply with the rules of
government departments in order to benefit from state finance. Either
could have operated independently had it so wished.

With the passage of time both the *Mount Edgcumbe* and the School of
Navigation had to face the realisation that they were offering something
to the mercantile marine which it was not wholly interested in receiving.
The ideals of the founders of the *Mount Edgcumbe* were frustrated by the
demise of the seaman apprenticeship system and the failure of the
shipping industry to adopt any other system of training its seamen; there
was also the widespread unwillingness of owners to employ boys, noted
above. A further disadvantage was the association of the Ship with the
prison service which oversaw the industrial schools; it was difficult to
shake the idea that criminals were being offered as crew members for
merchant ships. For the promoters of the School of Navigation the ideal
of providing a broad nautical education was thwarted by the disinterest
of merchant marine officers in any education which was wider than that
needed to pass the masters and mates examinations. In addition the
School had not succeeded in running significant pre-sea courses.

How important was it that these two establishments should have
existed in Plymouth? The justification seems to be stronger for the
navigation school than for the ship. Many of the men of Devon and
Cornwall were seamen, and those that wished to advance their nautical
education were entitled to find a navigation school in the region's
leading port, especially once it had been granted a local marine board

and thus became an examination centre for Board of Trade examinations. Certainly once the private teachers of navigation had ceased to practise such a school was needed, but it is not possible to say whether the Plymouth School of Navigation was so successful that it put them out of business, or whether their main work was with naval personnel and that this source of students disappeared as the Navy developed its own system of education and training. Whether Devon and Cornwall really needed a training ship seems doubtful in view of the small number of boys it received from the area. Could it have been established more in the context of local prestige - that Plymouth should be seen to be contributing to the national effort?

In the context of social welfare the *Mount Edgcumbe* no doubt did useful work. For many of the 3301 boys who passed through the Ship during her existence she was 'home' and represented stability in a real sense.[1] Yet, as has been observed, even before she was founded doubts were being expressed publically about the suitability of old ships for this work. The *Endeavour,* a shore-based establishment at Feltham on the Thames, which was equipped with a full-scale model brig for training purposes, showed that an equally good pre-sea training could be provided in a more open and healthier environment on land.[2] By the end of the nineteenth century training ships were being viewed less favourably, mainly on the grounds of health and safety. Many of the ships were worn out, and they were not easy to replace without heavy expense. Some ships were closed down, but others, such as the *Formidable,* were able to raise the money to move into new accommodation on shore.

The *Mount Edgcumbe* did not make this transition. In 1910 the tender, *Goshawk,* was laid up as an economy measure and later sold. Yet during the last ten years of her existence the Ship enjoyed perhaps her most successful period, achieving a full complement of boys from 1912,[3] and sending a much larger proportion of boys to sea than previously. In 1913 the future of the Ship was discussed at the Home Office. Her certification was allowed to continue because:

> Mr Russell [Chief Inspector of Reformatory and Industrial Schools] feels that the present Captain is a good man and that there is nothing flagrantly wrong with the ship... they make a good case for retaining their ship school which now sends 90% of the boys to the Navy or the merchant service.[4]

By 1920 age and wartime neglect made a change of vessel essential. The Home Office offered £1500 to support a move to a new ship but would only guarantee a five-year extension of the certificate. The 'committing

1   *Naval and Military Record,* 2 February 1921, p.76.

2   Brassey, *British seamen,* p.49.

3   T.S. *Mount Edgcumbe,* 41st annual report, p.16.

4   PRO HO 45/11051/155236.

72

authority' had to match this sum.[1] The *Mount Edgcumbe* committee found
the conditions too restrictive and decided to resign the certificate
and return the ship to the Admiralty. She was broken up at Queen
Anne's Battery, Coxside, the site on which the School of Navigation
Seamanship Centre was built in 1967.

For the first half of the twentieth century the Plymouth School
of Navigation continued to prepare candidates for the masters and mates
examinations. In 1908, with the ending of the Science and Art grants
and the demise of local marine boards, its management was passed to the
local education authority.[2] In 1922 the school moved to larger premises
in Durnford Street, and in the same year a move at a meeting of the
Education Committee to close it down on the grounds of expense was
successfully resisted.[3] In 1932 the School became a department of the
Plymouth and Devonport Technical College and there followed a very lean
period, when enrolments dropped to as low as 28 in 1935-6.[4] Between
1932 and 1954, when it moved to the top floor of the new college
building, the School occupied a variety of premises. Its recovery
commenced in 1949 with the establishment of a pre-sea officer cadet
course, in addition to the classes for masters and mates. Thereafter
a variety of nautical courses was started, including those for engineer
cadets and a degree course in nautical studies. In 1964 a training
ketch was acquired, and in 1967 its well-developed seamanship and boat-
work classes moved to Coxside. The education and training of Merchant
Navy cadets had become a residential activity, and in 1970 the school
acquired purpose-built residential and teaching accommodation. In the
same year the College, by then a College of Technology, was divided to
create Plymouth Polytechnic and the College of Further Education, the
cadet courses going to the latter, masters and mates courses and degree
courses to the former. Thus a hundred years after the Department of
Science and Art nationally, and John Merrifield locally, had aspired to
broadly-based nautical courses, they were being offered in Plymouth.

1   PRO HO 45/11051, 155236.

2   Fifth annual report of the Plymouth Education Committee, 1908.

3   Minutes of the Plymouth Education Committee, 25 May 1922.

4   School of Navigation registers.

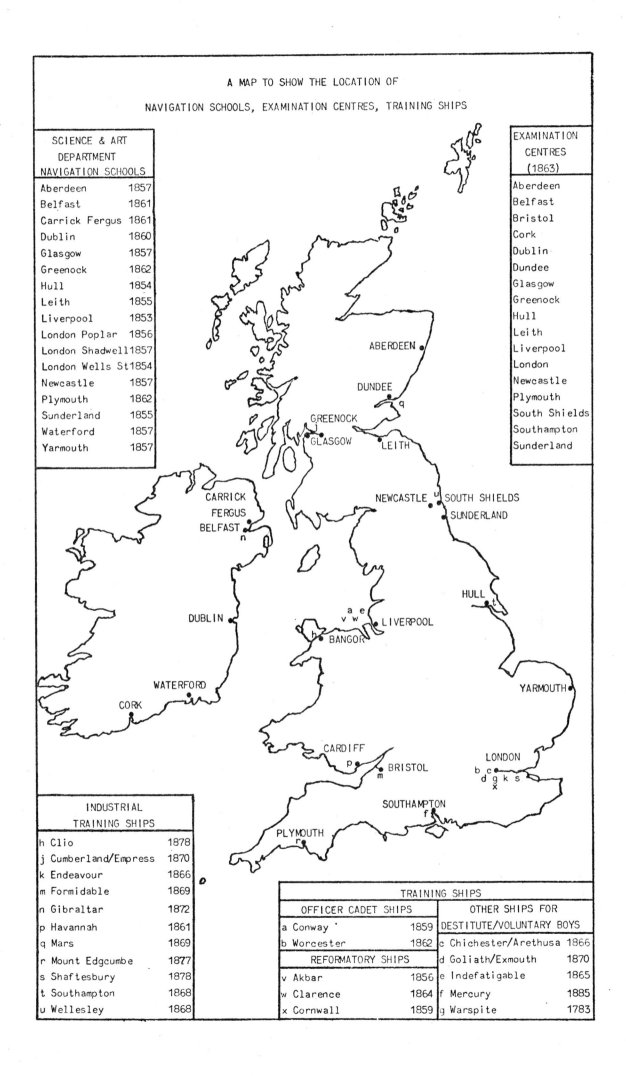

A MAP TO SHOW THE LOCATION OF

NAVIGATION SCHOOLS, EXAMINATION CENTRES, TRAINING SHIPS

SCIENCE & ART DEPARTMENT NAVIGATION SCHOOLS

Aberdeen	1857
Belfast	1861
Carrick Fergus	1861
Dublin	1860
Glasgow	1857
Greenock	1862
Hull	1854
Leith	1855
Liverpool	1853
London Poplar	1856
London Shadwell	1857
London Wells St	1854
Newcastle	1857
Plymouth	1862
Sunderland	1855
Waterford	1857
Yarmouth	1857

EXAMINATION CENTRES (1863)

Aberdeen
Belfast
Bristol
Cork
Dublin
Dundee
Glasgow
Greenock
Hull
Leith
Liverpool
London
Newcastle
Plymouth
South Shields
Southampton
Sunderland

INDUSTRIAL TRAINING SHIPS

h	Clio	1878
j	Cumberland/Empress	1870
k	Endeavour	1866
m	Formidable	1869
n	Gibraltar	1872
p	Havannah	1861
q	Mars	1869
r	Mount Edgcumbe	1877
s	Shaftesbury	1878
t	Southampton	1868
u	Wellesley	1868

TRAINING SHIPS

OFFICER CADET SHIPS		OTHER SHIPS FOR DESTITUTE/VOLUNTARY BOYS		
a Conway	1859			
b Worcester	1862	c Chichester/Arethusa	1866	
REFORMATORY SHIPS		d Goliath/Exmouth	1870	
v Akbar	1856	e Indefatigable	1865	
w Clarence	1864	f Mercury	1885	
x Cornwall	1859	g Warspite	1783	

Drawing of John Merrifield in the *Western Figaro*,
8 January 1880

13½ Gascoyn Place, Plymouth, the first home
of the Plymouth School of Navigation

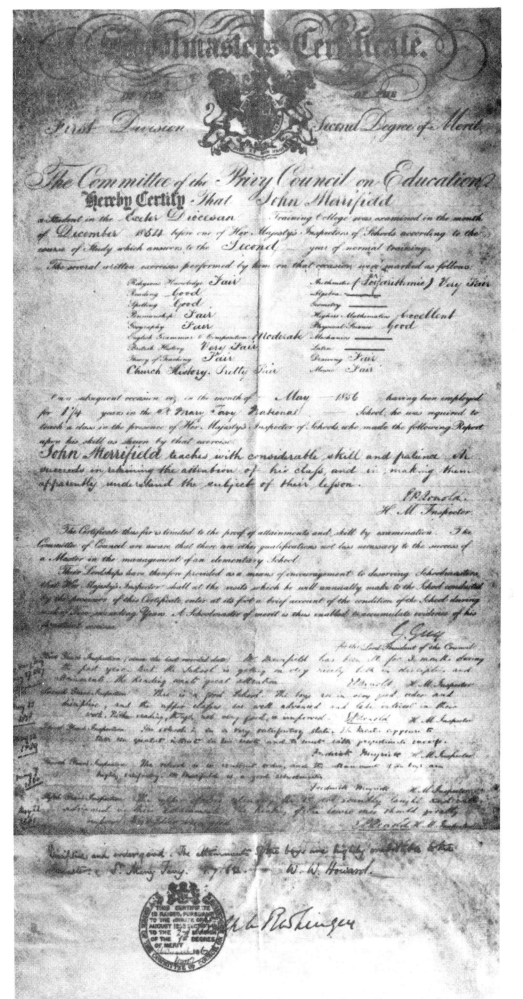

John Merrifield's teaching certificate, 1862

T.S. *Mount Edgcumbe*, c.1916 (photograph kindly provided by Mrs F Parcelle)

Divisions on T.S. *Mount Edgcumbe*, c.1916
(photograph kindly provided by Mrs F Parcelle)

Training Ship "Mount Edgcumbe,"

LYING OFF SALTASH.

This is to Certify that _Alfred Smith_ has served on board this Ship from the _7th June_ 1910 to the date hereof.

PROFICIENCY AND CONDUCT.

STANDARD		
READING	Good	
WRITING	Good	
ARITHMETIC	Good	
REPAIRING CLOTHES	Very Good	
SWIMMING	Very Good	

KNOTTING, SPLICING AND BENDS	Very Good
LEAD AND COMPASS	Very Good
PALM AND NEEDLE	Very Good
MANAGING A BOAT UNDER OARS	Very Good
ACTIVITY ALOFT	Very Good

CONDUCT DURING LAST YEAR'S SERVICE _Very Good_

Given under my hand on board the "Mount Edgcumbe," off Saltash, this _1st_ day of _June_ 19_12_

Aug. Weston

{ Captain-Superintendent.

AGE ON DISCHARGE. } _16 Years_

Leaving Certificate of the T.S. _Mount Edgcumbe_, 1912

SHIPS' ENGINEERS:

THEIR STATUS AND POSITION ON BOARD, c.1830-65

H. Campbell McMurray

I have often been astonished when reading books on sea life, to observe that notwithstanding the enormous strides made in propelling machinery during the last half-century, so little has been written about the inner life of the men who design, control and maintain them, and who have achieved so truly a wonderful a revolution in all that pertains to a life on the ocean wave.[1]

If we were to attempt to gauge the role of ships' engineers over the last century or so, by comparing the amount of autobiographical matter and personal memoirs they have generated with that vast mountain of words bequeathed to posterity by deck officers and shipmasters, we would conclude that their role had been of almost indecently negligible proportions.[2] However, the varying tendency of nautical men to put pen to paper cannot be taken seriously as an indicator of roles and importance.[3] But should we then turn to the more general maritime literature we might well feel that the place of the 'black gang' in the general order of things has enjoyed a less than full consideration.

Lord Brassey, for instance, makes only passing reference in all his numerous writings on the mercantile shipping industry to the fact that ships might carry engineers, and then it is only to comment on their propensity to consume strong drink.[4] Cornewall-Jones, in 400 pages or so devoted but one-half of one page to a description of their activities, while giving over entire chapters to each of the following: the masters, the deck officers, the deck apprentices, the deck crew, and their respective work tasks.[5] While Clement Jones was barely able to lend the engine-room crowd a mention in his

1   Peter L Waldron, *Afloat and ashore: the reminiscences of a marine engineer* (Leith: G C McKay, n.d. but c.1917) preface.

2   Other engineers than Waldron to have written of their experiences include William G Riddell, *Adventures of an obscure Victorian* (Macmillan, 1932), Warren Armstrong, *Saltwater tramp* (Jarrolds, 1944), and John Lamb, *Backward thinking* (Wallsend: J Thompson, 1954).

3   The apparent literary reticence of marine engineers is a complicated matter. Moreover, such reasons as may be adduced lie rather outside the scope of this discussion, in the area of education, class and opportunity, and in the extent to which the shore-side system of social stratification and its structure of opportunities penetrates and shapes the pattern of recruitment into shipboard occupations. On this see, Peter H Fricke, *The social structure of the crews of dry cargo ships* (Cardiff: UWIST, 1974) p.167 ff.

4   Thomas Brassey, *British seamen* (Longmans Green, 1877) p.296, reporting the opinion of the British consul at Santander, 30 June 1875.

5   Richard J Cornewall-Jones, *The British merchant service* (Sampson, Low, Marston, 1898) p.275.

index, and, quite unbelievably, could dismiss the largest proportion
of their work in a mere two lines - to the effect that 'their duties
are obvious to anyone who has ever visited the furnaces or boiler-
house of a factory'.[1] Frank Bullen, in his tribute to the men of the
merchant navy, as could have been expected, does rather better by the
engineers; here, both they and the engine-room hands each have a
chapter devoted to their doings.[2] Disappointingly, while quite a
strong feeling is displayed for the world down below, as the author
himself owns, he is not sufficiently well-versed in the subject to go
much beyond a restatement of some fairly predictable, if to the
uninitiated not at all obvious, generalities. Little further enlighten-
ment will be found in the formal technical histories of marine
engineering,[3] where the concern is with the machinery and not with those
responsible for its operation. More useful, probably, are the works of
authors like A E Seaton and R Sennet, whose magisterial manuals of
instruction and advice for young engineers preparing for their Board of
Trade examinations provide some fragments out of which can be built something of a picture of the working environment, duties and position of the
ship's engineer of the later nineteenth century.[4] Otherwise, engineers
of the period are perhaps best served by Edward Blackmore in what is in
effect a summary of papers presented to the Shipmasters' Society, a
professional association founded by and for serving shipmasters, during
the 1890s.[5] Perusal of this volume, and of the original papers of the
society,[6] show that the relative prominence of the engineers in these

1   *British merchant shipping* (Edward Arnold, 1922) p.117.

2   Frank T Bullen, *The men of the merchant service* (Smith Elder, 1900),
     chaps XXXIII and XXXIV.

3   In, for example, Edgar C Smith, *A short history of marine
     engineering* (Cambridge UP, 1937); or John Guthrie, *A history of
     marine engineering* (Hutchinson, 1971).

4   Alexander E Seaton, *A manual of marine engineering* (Charles Griffin,
     1888, 7th ed.); Richard Sennet, *The marine steam engine* (Longmans
     Green, 1885). From a slightly different viewpoint, perhaps as
     rounded a portrait of the ship's engineer as any is found in the
     works of Kipling - always an admirer, as Lionel Trilling remarked,
     of the 'technical, secret-laden adults who run the world, the
     overalled people, majestic in their occupation, superb in their
     pre-occupation, the dour engineer, the thoughtful plumber'. So,
     in his poem 'MacAndrew's Hymn', he succeeds in conveying just
     precisely that 'gallus' style affected by a certain kind of ship's
     engineer, and in capturing their somewhat pawky acceptance, as a
     breed, of a subordinate status on board the ship while yet deftly
     laying open the matter of their professional detachment from
     affairs nautical. The sea tales of James Hanley are also valuable,
     particularly those treating of firemen and trimmers, whereas Eugene
     O'Neill's *The hairy ape* is best considered separately, as a rather
     different specimen.

5   Edward Blackmore, *The British mercantile marine* (Charles Griffin, 1897).

6   *Transactions of the Shipmasters' Society* (1890-99).

texts is a fairly precise function of their expanding responsibilities on board and, accordingly, of their steady usurpation of that area of competence formerly occupied by the masters themselves.

To be fair it is just possible to perceive a certain chronological development in the treatment given to ships' engineers by the maritime chroniclers, the space and attention accorded tending to their favour as we come forward in time and as the growth of their responsibilities and their contribution to the efficient performance of the ship becomes more evident. Yet at no time are they over-represented. Even today, the growth of 'maritime ethnology' has not succeeded in altering the engineers' place in the scheme of things to any marked extent. Thus, where analysis is directed to the study of men in ships, as opposed to the more general study of life in maritime communities, the great burden of enquiry hitherto has tended to concentrate on life and work in the old sailing ships. This pre-occupation with a dying culture is perfectly reasonable. Sailing ship traffic, as Henning Henningsen writes, 'is decidedly something that demands research, because it is now an almost closed chapter'. But, as he goes on to point out in the same paragraph:

> ...it would be quite wrong to draw a line across the page and write FINIS. In our own time, we see that the day of the steam-ship - at any rate, the coal-fired ship - is nearly over, and the period of the motor ship is certain, sooner or later, to draw to a close. Collection of material and research should also, there-fore, include the culture in these mechanically-propelled ships ... Likewise, it is of the greatest interest to give an account of the effects, both the material and the psychological, that the change-over from sail to machinery had on the seamen who experienced this.[1]

We concur. The purpose of the present paper, then, is to offer some observations on the opening phase of this transition from Neptune to Vulcan, with special reference to the position and circumstances on board ship of the early marine engine operators. Employing as a rough point of reference the problem of the 'status of the engineer' on shipboard, and bearing in mind the relatively unpropitious circumstances attending the advent of the mechanical prime mover at sea, discussion will focus on the sources of recruitment in the early period; on the kinds of problems - economic, social, occupational - posed for the orthodox sailorman by the carriers of the new technology and the object of their attentions; and on the status and position on board first assigned to these 'rude mechanicals'; with some tentative suggestions as to how these matters were perceived by the engineers themselves.

1   Henning Henningsen, 'The life of the sailor afloat and ashore', in O Hasslof, H Henningsen and A Christiansen, jr., eds. *Ships and shipyards, sailors and fishermen* (Copenhagen: Rosenkilde & Baggen, 1972) pp.138-9.

II

With the introduction of steam navigation early in the nineteenth
century, a new class of seafarer emerged: the marine engineer. In
the strong, capable, if oft dirty hands of this new breed lay the
responsibility for the running and maintenance of the ship's machinery.
It cannot be said, however, that these pioneers comprised an altogether
indispensable element in the well-being of British maritime commerce,
vital as their contribution was in due course to become, for, although
grand enough to be sure, the early steamship was but a modest technical
triumph, enjoying at first only a limited commercial success.

There is no need here to rehearse the long, complicated history of
steam navigation, but what should not go unnoticed is the fact that the
transition from sail to steam did not take place overnight. Thus, in
the 1830s the machine was still hardly more than a jumble of restive
horses, the stuttering quality of whose performance was reflected in
the strictly limited purposes for which the steamship was employed and
in the slow growth, if not in its numbers, in the total amount of steam-
propelled tonnage annually being added to the registers. In 1820, there
were 34 steamers on the official British register, totalling some 3,000
tons; by 1830, the number had risen to around 298, making up around
30,000 tons; ten years later, 771 steamers had been placed on the
register, of a total tonnage slightly in excess of 87,000.[1] Only in the
1840s do we encounter anything resembling a successful bulk-carrying
steamship; even by 1860 or so the steamer was still largely confined to
river, coastal and harbour work and to the shorter sea routes. On routes
where passenger traffic, mails and baggage comprised the largest share of
the trade, together with high value, perishable cargoes such as fruit and
dairy produce, the steamer introduced a speedy, year-round reliability of
service which the sailing ship, tied to the elements could not provide.[2]
In this area of business, where coal costs, varying inversely with the
length of voyage from the principal and cheapest source of supply, Britain,
were of comparatively minor account, the steamship, in conjunction with the
railway, quickly developed a market for its services. In these shorter
trades the steamship was of advantage too in the savings made in insurance and interest of money, together with the added facility it
offered of a normal dependence on a given number of days for a passage.
In the broad ocean trades, conversely, the steamer for long could not
compete.[3] Here, the superb sailing ship of the 1860s and 1870s, bigger

1   Brian R Mitchell and Phyllis Deane, *Abstract of British historical
     statistics* (Cambridge UP, 1962) pp.217-9; *Board of Trade statistical
     abstracts for the U.K.*, 1830-54, C 144, Table 26, p.59.

2   The widespread adoption of the steam tug-boat of course served to
     repair this basic deficiency of the sailing ship, and to prolong
     its utility as a cargo carrier.

3   Charles K Harley, 'The shift from sailing ships to steamships: a
     study of technological change and its diffusion' in D McCloskey,
     ed. *Essays on a mature economy* (Methuen, 1972) pp.215-31, *passim*.

and faster than her predecessors, with proportionately more cargo space per cubic ton, and better manned with fewer men, retained a predominance practically comparable with that of the steamer in the short-haul business.[1] And to around 1870 or so, it is almost only in the government-sponsored mail packet services, chiefly for passengers, that we find the steamer making any serious inroads into the monopoly in ocean transport held by the sailing vessel.[2]

Given, then, the still limited extent of the employment of steam propulsion in commerce to the 1860s, we will consider the possible sources of recruitment of the engineers themselves.

Obviously, in the early days of steam at sea, until about 1840, the numbers coming forward with experience of operating any kind of running plant could not have been high. The supply of such men as were available, moreover, seems quickly to have become exhausted. As one of the witnesses speaking before the Select Committee on Steamboat Accidents of 1839 put it:

> [steam navigation] has advanced more rapidly than men of experience and knowledge can be found to conduct it; hence, we often find, in the river packets in particular, men advanced to the post of engineer who are mere automatons, ignorant of the first principles of the machinery over which they preside who, in case of any derangement, do from ignorance of the result the very thing which they ought to have avoided, creating rather than averting danger or accident.[3]

Some at least of these early 'engineers', and probably a majority of the firemen and trimmers, came from the ranks of the sailors; others could have been recruited from one or other of the shore-side crafts adversely affected during the period by the growth of factory-based, machine production, or from among other groups of the unemployed – as evidently was the case with the first railway foot-platemen. The two callings possessed a number of features in common: the steam engine was the revolutionary innovation of its day and represented, in both cases, an application of power technology to a mode of activity till then more or less reliant on natural resources; both jobs required from their adherents a degree of technical knowhow, or an interest in things mechanical, some reasonable grasp of the principles governing the safe operation and working of running machinery and a generally disciplined approach to the work. Both occupations, in short, needed men of 'great activity and ability to get out of a difficulty'.[4] For the railways,

1   Gerald S Graham, 'The ascendancy of the sailing ship', *Economic History Review*, 2nd series, IX (1956) 74-88.

2   It may be said, moreover, that without the mail contracts the new steam packet companies of the later 1830s and 1840s – P & O, Royal West Indian Mail and the like – could hardly have continued with their operations. Harold J Dyos and Derek H Aldcroft, *British transport: an economic history from the 17th to the 20th century* (Leicester UP, 1969) chap. 8. *passim*.

3   *BPP*, 1839, XLVII, 18, Report of the Select Committee on Steamboat Accidents, evidence of Edward Gibson, p.109.

4   Peter W Kingsford, *Victorian railwaymen: the emergence and growth of railway labour, 1830-1870* (Frank Cass, 1970) p.5.

as Kingsford has written, this type of man might hail from anywhere, where he could be found at all:

> In the thirties and forties the demand for them was greater than the supply; they could 'dictate their own terms in great degree'. It was difficult to get skilful and reliable men. They were recruited not from blacksmiths, as one member of the 1839 Select Committee [on the railways] supposed, but mainly from labourers who showed an aptitude for the work ... Brunel considered it an advantage if they were illiterate,[1] and many of them were so. A few no doubt ... came directly to the company from the decaying handloom weavers and without the advantage of schooling...[2]

Broadly speaking, railway engine-men were not expected to display more than a rudimentary knowledge of their engines, nor as a rule were they required to carry out running repairs or attend to routine maintenance, whereas ships' engineers had to be competent in such matters. Thus, writing in the 1890s on the subject of engineers in the early home trade steamers, Edward Blackmore, a former master mariner, took a more optimistic view of their capabilities than the one purveyed by the witnesses before the Select Committee on Steamboat Accidents. A very large number, he wrote:

> had not served an apprenticeship in the trade but were engine drivers raised from the shovel - many of them good, steady fellows who handled well the slow-going machinery of the times, with its low pressures - most of them a good deal better than a chance engineer out of a shop put in charge of machinery afloat with little or no experience as a sea-going engineer.[3]

Altogether, an exceedingly home-spun race, yet who in default of a ready made supply of more suitably qualified men, in all likelihood answered the purpose well enough in the coasting steamers, which in case of emergency were never far from assistance.

However, where voyages were of more extended duration, as from the later 1830s or so with the rise of the bigger mail packets, a rather more intimate acquaintance with the construction, maintenance and repair of the steam engine was called for. Thus, Blackmore again:

1   Quite why Brunel preferred unlettered engine-drivers is not clear, but interestingly enough, Messrs Forrester and McGregor, Engineers, of Liverpool, in their submission to the Committee on steamboat accidents stated that they 'preferred and recommended labourers rather than mechanics as engineers in steamboats, for the reason that mechanics would frequently not endure them, being liable to be treated as seamen by the captains'. *BPP*, 1839, XLVII, 18, p.65.

2   Kingsford, *Victorian railwaymen*, pp.4-5.

3   Blackmore, *Mercantile marine*, p.172.

'... in our first class steamers, the engineers have from the start been hand-picked men'.[1] As like as not, men with little experience of the sea, but familiar with engine-building and repair shops ashore, and typically appointed in the first instance on the recommendation of the engine maker. This is reasonable: these men were required to handle with skill and address, for the time, very large pieces of machinery - limping giants of doubtful efficiency and temperamental disposition - and to be responsible for their functioning in what would often be isolated and perilous circumstances. From the outset, then, it would appear that the engineers employed in the bigger, foreign-going steamers - and it is those working in the larger, deep-water vessels with whom we are mainly concerned - seem likely to have been skilled craftspeople, drawn, it may be hazarded, from that flourishing aristocracy of nineteenth century labour, 'the engineers' - though not a few in the earlier period might have been more familiarly known as millwrights, or similar. And in their careful analysis of 'the inquiry into the rules and regulations of the trade in all districts of the country' conducted by the Amalgamated Society of Engineers, in 1861, M and J B Jefferys could be read as suggesting something of the kind.[2] Thus, in a discussion of weekly earnings in the trade at that time, they point out that these 'ranged from 18/- in Hayle, Cornwall, where 56 engineers were engaged on "all kinds of steam engine and mill work", to 36/6 paid to members of the Tower Hamlets branch, in London, who specialized in marine engine work'.[3] Several factors accounted for these wage variations: for instance, rates were fixed locally, almost on a shop to shop basis, while the higher cost of living in London would have played some part in lifting earnings there. In this connection perhaps of most importance was the type of work undertaken:

> The members in the London branches and in the large branches in south eastern England such as Brighton and Ashford were chiefly engaged in marine and locomotive work... Marine engineering and, to a lesser extent, locomotive engineering, were at this date highly skilled trades employing the best craftsmen.[4]

Now, it is true, these remarks are made in reference to shore-side trades-men; perhaps it was the duds who went to sea! This is not likely, how-ever, and although at present in support of this contention only a handful of partial, rather imperfect biographical sketches of con-temporary ships' engineers, can be brought forward, it seems that there was at the least a good mix, with competent, skilled men in the majority.

Let us now consider the kind of reception accorded the first sea-going engineers on board the larger vessels, the status and position

1   Blackmore, *Mercantile marine,* p.172.

2   M & J B Jefferys, 'The wages, hours and trade customs of the skilled engineer in 1861', *Economic History Review,* 1st series, XVIII (1948) 27-44.

3   Jefferys, 'Skilled engineer', p.33.

4   Jefferys, 'Skilled engineer' p.33.

assigned them in the shipboard hierarchy, and, by way of inference, the way that this might have been perceived by the engineers themselves.

On this question we shall employ the concept of 'relative deprivation', an idea first used by the authors of a study of American combat troops in the Second World War[1] in an attempt to interpret an odd lack of congruence between certain types of experiences and the reactions thereby engendered. The idea may be stated briefly: the reactions of any group or category of persons to hardships experienced by them will tend to vary in intensity according to the differences between their situation and that of other groups with whom they compare themselves; it varies, in other words, according to their choice of 'reference group'.[2] Deprivation clearly implies a sense of inequity, relative in that it varies in respect of some social standard internalized in the shape of aspirations or self-expectations; one who is 'relatively deprived', however, need not be 'objectively deprived' in the broader sense that he is lacking in some minimum, necessary standard of comfort, though the likelihood will be that he has not previously enjoyed whatever the 'deprivation' is imagined to be.[3] Then, obviously, in order for the members of one, less well-placed group somehow to feel themselves to be deprived in comparison with what they imagine to be the situation of another group, there must be perceived in the first place at least a common point of reference, some feeling of similarity of status attributes between the two groups: only thus, it will be evident, can a sense of relative deprivation be aroused and the comparisons drawn.[4] In fine, relative deprivation denotes the feeling of hardship, grievance or injustice which emerges through the agency of this comparison.

Reverting to the matter at hand, in numerous ways the advent of the steamship meant for the seafarer improved employment prospects and, in the longer term, better conditions. For instance, ships now carried larger numbers of crew, and not only engineers but firemen too. Engineers and firemen had uncongenial work perhaps but work that was better paid than deck work, and with watches arranged on a four hours on/eight hours off basis, against four on/four off on deck. In terms of the overall demand for shipping and the consequent growth of employment opportunities for the sea-going labour force, steam gave a decided stimulus. It may be said too that mail steamers, sailing against time, with a regularity sometimes beyond the demands of seasonal

1   Samuel A Stouffer, *et al*, *The American soldier, I: adjustment during army life* (Princeton UP, 1949) p.125 ff.

2   Though the organising principle had been lurking around for many years Herbert H Hyman, 'The psychology of status', *Archives of Psychology*, 259 (New York, 1942), was the first to use the term.

3   Walter G Runciman, *Relative deprivation and social justice* (Routledge Kegan Paul, 1966) Chap. 2 *passim*.

4   Robert K Merton and Alice S Rossi, 'Contributions to the theory of reference group behaviour', in Robert K Merton, ed. *Social theory and social structure* (Glencoe, Illinois: The Free Press, 1957) p.242.

trade, offered the seafarer the possibility of more continuous employment in larger, better-found, stauncher ships.[1]

In spite of these effects, however, it seems that the early ships'
engineers did encounter a certain resistance from the sailors.[2] It
must be remembered that the first ocean steamers were dirty, noisy,
smoky little craft whose wheezing, croaking, groaning machinery laboured
to produce only a modest, unpredictable action, so much so, indeed, that
in the opening years of steam navigation, and for long afterwards, steamships were built heavily masted, fully rigged and equipped with such a
sufficiency of sail as would render them more or less independent of
their engines. Add to this, the murderous quarrel taking place between
primitive technologies and scientific principles, and its occasional
accompaniment, the sudden, clattering thunder of bursting boilers, and
there was much to reinforce the obstinately held convictions of those
who had determined that steam was out of place at sea. Conceivably, on
the part of the old sailormen, their assessment of the matter was not a
little influenced by their distaste for, and distrust of, any innovation,
especially one which some of the more shrewd among them must have grasped
as having the potential to appropriate that area of competence which
custom and tradition had ordained as their own. Clearly the influx of
the 'rude mechanicals' posed a complex threat to the orthodox sailor and
to the traditional stability of the shipboard organization. In the days
of the sailing ship, the master, the mates and the crew always and at
all times had perforce to control and propel the vessel in the best way
they could by manipulating arrays of canvas in a variety of ingenious
ways. In a sense, therefore, to deprive seamen of this role, as the
marine engine even in its earliest form must have looked capable of
doing, was to take away the largest part of the individual seafarer's
raison d'être. In different words, through the enforced obsolescence of
skills:

> labour saving technology produces acute psychological and social
> problems for the worker. The difficulty does not lie exclusively
> in the need for learning new routines of work. The need for
> discarding acquired skills and, often, the accompanying demotion
> of status destroys the positive self-image of the worker stemming
> from the confident use of those skills.[3]

1   The steamship was an expensive item of capital and required, if it
    was to offer any kind of challenge in its early days to the sailing
    vessel on the oceans, a premium trading pattern. This, alongside
    the need to provide coal supplies and repair facilities, was among
    the factors which encouraged more regular, predictable voyaging, so
    enhancing the seafarer's opportunity for more continuous employment.
    See, Francis E Hyde, *Blue funnel* (Liverpool UP, 1957) Chap. 1,
    passim.

2   Similar problems were encountered by the first radio operators at
    sea. See Jane C Record, 'The marine radio-man's struggle for
    status', *American Journal of Sociology*, 63, 1 (1957).

3   Robert K Merton, 'The machine, the worker and the engineer', in
    Merton, *Social theory*, p.343.

On the question of this likely violation of the seafarer's occupational self-esteem wrought by the advent of mechanical propulsion at sea, it is pertinent to note that the seaman's work, as has often been suggested, tends to penetrate the inner life of the man to such an extent as may be said to 'contaminate the personality'. A seaman, that is to say:

> ...is what he is and does what he does, ashore as on shipboard, not so much because he is a given type of person but rather because he has a certain kind of job. Few other industries are able to match the merchant marine in terms of its profound effects upon the entire life pattern of its workers, away from work as well as on duty.[1]

The merchant seaman is thus the prisoner of his occupational status to an extraordinary degree. Arguably, therefore, to introduce changes here was to seek, if unknowingly, to alter rather more than the mere extent of the proposed change itself. Under such circumstances, the longer a man has been to sea, the greater will tend to be his commitment to the work and to the structure of sentiments arising therefrom: these largely comprise his universe. Any attempt to revolutionize the character of the work constitutes a threat not only to the individual vocational identity but, on account of the peculiarly over-extended nature of the commitment to the occupation, to the whole person, to a man's very conception of himself. It was liable therefore, one may surmise, to have been resisted. And perhaps vigorously. For in this context it is not impossible that there were instances of 'machine breaking' by the sailors of a vessel's machinery during the early phase of steam navigation.[2] If such occurrences took place, the likelihood would be that they were less an example of 'collective bargaining by riot', but, rather, owed their provenance to the problems associated with the assault on the sailorman's conception of himself which the new machinery posed.[3]

1   Elmo P Hohman, *Seamen ashore: a study of the united seamen's service and of merchant seamen in port* (Yale UP, 1952), p. xv.

2   Cf Eric J Hobsbawm, 'The machine breakers', in his *Labouring men: studies in the history of labour* (Weidenfeld & Nicolson, 1964, 1968) pp. 5-22.

3   Vilhelm Aubert and Oddvar Arner, 'On the social structure of the ship', *Acta Sociologica*, 3 (1959) 200-19. Thus, drawing attention to his occupation and place on board, the authors state that 'this may give us a certain perspective on the reception which the first engineers got on board ships - and perhaps also an explanation of the traditional teasing relationship between deck and engine. The engine represented a totally strange element on board, and the engineers represented a clear threat to the occupational identity of the deck crew and officers. Because the engineers were not seamen, and did not know the seamen's work, they were called coal shovellers and etc. If they were to be taken as seamen, the concept of the seaman would become dangerously unclear and the identity of the seaman could not very well tolerate such a challenge to the traditional demarcation'.

Possibly as a result of these strains, though it is more likely
to have been determined by the degree of importance attached to their
duties by the old-time nautical autocracy, the carriers of the new
technology seem to have been allotted a place in the shipboard hierarchy
roughly congruent with that of the other tradesmen on board, notably the
sailmaker and the carpenter. Such a position was some way removed from
what their future contribution was to reveal would have been appropriate.
Yet as operators of a new and untried device the long term success of
which could not initially be assured, it was by no means inappropriate.
It must be said here that given the kind of evidence we have been able
to appraise so far, the precise dimensions of social standing and status
on shipboard at this lower level - except for what may be deduced from
wage data or ships' plans in which living and dining arrangements are
shown, and amplified by impressions from a variety of sources - can be
very difficult to establish. Certain interpretations of the evidence
indeed tend to place the engineers more on a footing with the ordinary
sailors.

In the event, as the author of the history of the Institute of
Marine Engineers was moved to remark, in the early days of mechanical
propulsion at sea, the machinery was in the charge of 'artisans with
little or no technical education or social qualifications'.[1] Arguably
true enough, though the implications do rather less than justice to
the subtleties connoted by the term 'artisan' in the nineteenth century
vernacular.[2] But his general drift is clear and intuitively convincing,
viz. the first engineers to serve at sea were remiss in the sort of
personal and professional qualities which might have enabled them to
lay claim to a superior status on shipboard. The concept of 'status'
in shipboard totemism, it may be noted in passing, in addition to its
orthodox components - prestige, social standing and so on - as an
index of rank on board connotes one further, important element, that
of authority and its ensuing prerogatives. Thus, assuming our estimate
to be more or less correct, that at the commencement of steam navigation
in the merchant service engineers were granted a type of petty officer
status, this comparatively elevated position within the system of shipboard stratification, somewhat above that of the common sailors but not
quite on a par with the navigators, taken together with such appurtenant
privileges as that obtained, might, one would argue, have been thought
acceptable to the majority of these early mechanics in that it offered
them a position roughly corresponding with their contribution to the
performance of the ship which, with the faltering success of the innovation at the first, was not always of paramount importance. At the
same time, while the engineer had charge of the engine-room and was seen
as the responsible man there, the somewhat qualified nature of his
duties, in comparison with the all-embracing responsibilities of, for
example, the first mate, the chief executive officer on board,

1   Bernard C Curling, *The history of the Institute of Marine Engineers*
     (Eyre & Spottiswoode, 1965) p.3.

2   As is well known, and as, for instance, Musson writes, 'another
     distinguishing feature of these skilled artisans was their general
     literacy. Many had some schooling while others had performed
     feats of self-education'. Albert E Musson, *British trade unions,
     1800-1875* (Macmillan, 1972) p.18.

the representative in almost everything of the master and, in law,
his successor, with responsibility for the upkeep of the ship, the
working of the crew, the stowage, safe-keeping and delivery of the
cargo, and so on, must, one would submit, have played a significant
part in the formation of attitudes among engineers toward their
status and right to wield influence on board during this period.
Indeed, engineers may be thought to have had some grounds for satis-
faction with the position as it was, for in addition to the fact that
their services could scarcely be described as indispensable in every
case, the majority of engineers in the sea service at this time,
owing to the poor supply of them and perhaps also to their better
organisation ashore, were actually earning rather higher wages than
the great number of deck officers, save the masters. Evidence for
this before 1840 is sketchy: but examination of Crew Lists and
Articles of Agreement for the period, and of the records of one or
two mail steamship companies, indicate that while great variations
existed the engineers consistently received more than all other crew-
men, if not as a rule the master or commander.[1]

1   '...the remuneration of engineers is greatly superior to that of
     deck officers, as the traditions of their calling have been much
     in their favour, the competition for employment not having been
     so severe as that of the sailor'. Blackmore, *Mercantile marine*,
     p.172. In one of a number of investigations to which the postal
     services, the mail packets in particular, were subjected in the
     1830s, rates of pay for sea staff were given as follows:
     Commander, £280 pa; Chief Mate, £6 pm; Second Mate, £3.14s pm;
     Engineer, £8.8s pm; Carpenter, £3.10s pm; ABs, £3.5s pm; Firemen,
     £4.4s pm; Steward, £1.17s pm. These moneys are quoted with
     reference to the Irish sea and cross-channel packet service,
     where provisions were not found; incidentally, at no point in the
     report (Append. C), is it suggested that engineers were required
     to pay their assistants, firemen and oilers, as was often the
     case with the railways at this time. Sixth Report of the Comm-
     issioners into the Management of the Post Office Department, *BPP*,
     1836, XXVIII, Append. F, No.2, p.194. In the Peninsular &
     Oriental Steam Navigation Company's ship *Oriental,* on a passage
     from Southampton to Calcutta, wage rates for the crew per month
     included the following: Commander £33.6s (plus allowances);
     Chief Officer, £15; Second Officer, £12; Third Officer, £9; the
     First Engineer, £25; Second Engineer £16; Third Engineer £14.
     National Maritime Museum, P & O S.N. Co., Board Minutes, P & O
     3/1. A partial examination of crew lists and articles of agree-
     ment indicates that not only does the same trend hold for engineers,
     but even the seamen in steamers seemed to be on a better rate than
     those in sail. PRO BT98, Muster rolls and articles of agreement,
     1744-1860. Brassey also notes that 'wages were as six in steam to
     five in sail'. Brassey, *British seamen,* p.163.

Our present impression is that while the deck officers seem to
have become in time, certainly in respect of the question of status
on board, the engineers' primary comparative reference group and the
focus on their part of aggrieved feelings of status deprivation,
during the opening decades of steam navigation, from the 1830s to
about 1860, this was probably not the case. Neither in terms of
the position occupied by them in the shipboard hierarchy nor from
the viewpoint of earnings, taken either relatively or absolutely,
can the first engineers to serve at sea be considered to have had
grounds for a strong sense of grievance vis-à-vis others on board.
What we may call the normative expectations of these early engineers
were not such as to have produced from them aspirations to executive
status on board: on the contrary, while engineers may have received
little encouragement to do so, pace Curling, neither at the time had
they a great deal of reason or incentive to identify with, and thus
to draw comparisons from, the altogether different situation of the
deck officers.

It is more likely, one feels, that the first wave of sea-going
engineers retained as their principal normative reference group the
artisan class in engineering ashore, and that they identified with
the range of assumptions, aspirations and grievances of this group
and drew comparisons accordingly. After all, in view of the relatively small number of sea-going engineers and their somewhat patchy
deployment across the handful of large companies then operating
steamers, it may be doubted whether there could have existed among
engineers a properly developed occupational consciousness of themselves as, specifically, a body of ships' engineers, with all that
that implies in terms of work group solidarity, community of outlook
and commitment to common action on their own behalf. At a time when
the marine prime mover had in no way realised its potential, perhaps
even seeming to many, especially at a time when deep-water sailing
ships had attained a new and striking supremacy,[1] as capable of only
limited application and of offering engineers, therefore, at best
limited career prospects, there might have been a great number who
would have considered it expedient to retain their craft ties and
other affiliations ashore. Furthermore, given that engineers,
possessing a set of skills which the orthodox sailorman lacked, enjoyed
a variety of alternative employment opportunities ashore, we can
assume, with some confidence, a good deal of movement between sea-
going and shoreside employment, men moving freely between engine-shops
on shore and ships at sea, some even coming ashore into more senior
positions within industry. The short point is that the engineer came
initially from ashore, ashore lay his chief sources of employment and
the basis of his economic strength and it was to there that he would
expect to return, sooner or later. To adopt Professor Phelps Brown's
description of the character and outlook of the craft-based trade
unionist of the period, the conditions in which engineers worked ashore

1   Graham, 'Sailing ship', *passim*.

were likely to have been of rather more interest to the sea-going
engineer than were those of people doing other jobs alongside him, and
too, in what for many may have been, on board ship, only a temporary
workplace.[1]

It may even be possible to argue that the early ships' engineers
occupied a position within the shipboard social structure not all that
far removed from that held by them in the wider society of mid-Victorian
England. That is to say, confining the discussion as we have done here-
tofore to the engineers in the larger mail packets, and holding to the
view that the largest number of these were probably skilled craftsmen,
members of the 'labour aristocracy', it might not be unreasonable to
suppose that like the builders, printers and bookbinders, for example,
of the older, pre-industrial crafts and ironworkers, foundrymen and
mechanics of all descriptions of the newer trades, they formed part of
that 'certain distinctive upper strata of the working class, better paid,
better treated, and generally regarded as more "respectable" and
politically moderate than the mass of the proletariat'.[2] Identifying
with, and largely included among, the lower middle class - a somewhat
fluid entity in nineteenth century England, one whose membership was
liable to change over time and according to geographical location, but
generally presumed to have included within its ranks the likes of small
shopkeepers, lower grade clerks,[3] minor masters, promoted workers like
foremen, as well as artisans - the prospects for the 'labour aristocracy'
of rising out of the artisan class and into a higher stratum, though
deteriorating throughout the century, remained far from negligible.[4]
Present though 'upward mobility strivings' undoubtedly were in the formation of attitudes among the artisan class at this time,[5] it is probably
wrong to attribute too much significance thereto: the essential
distinction then lay between the artisan and the unskilled labourer, one
which, as E P Thompson put it 'in terms of status, organisation and
economic reward - remained as great, if not greater, in Henry Mayhew's
London of the late 1840s and the 1850s as it was during the Napoleonic
Wars'.[6] The implications of this distinction were spelled out with

1   Edward H Phelps Brown, *The growth of British industrial relations:
    a study from the standpoint of 1906-1914* (Macmillan, 1959) p.118 ff.

2   Eric J Hobsbawm, 'The labour aristocracy in nineteenth century
    Britain', in his *Labouring men*, pp.272-315, p.272.

3   David Lockwood, *The blackcoated worker* (Unwin, 1958) Chap. 1,
    passim.

4   Sidney G Checkland, *The rise of industrial society in England,
    1815-1885* (Longmans Green, 1964).

5   Robert Q Gray, 'Styles of life: the "labour aristocracy" and
    class relations in later 19th century Edinburgh', *International
    Review of Social History*, 18 (1973) 428-52.

6   Edward P Thompson, *The making of the English working class*
    (Gollancz, rev. ed. 1968) p.266.

great succinctness by one worthy artisan:

> Between the artisan and the unskilled labourer a gulf is fixed.
> While the former resents the spirit in which he believes the
> followers of genteel occupations look down upon him, he in his
> turn looks down on the labourer. The artisan creed with regard
> to labourers is, that they are an inferior class, and that they
> should be made to know and kept in their place...[1]

Leaving aside the possibility of a revolutionary transformation
of the productive process, for at base the existence of a labour
aristocracy was founded on the archaic character of the early industrial
economy, the ability of this group to maintain its favoured position in
the class structure depended on exactly how successful it was in
controlling the supply of skilled labour into the trade. The New Model
Unions, craft-based combinations admitting only the most highly skilled
were, thus, essentially conservative groupings pursuing sectionalist
policies on entry, wages, hours, benefits, closed-shop agreements and
so on, aims more or less specifically designed to preserve their
members' aristocratic exclusiveness from the 'great residuum'. For a
while, at any rate, they were to achieve no small success. As Professor
Hobsbawm writes, relatively speaking:

> the position of the skilled artisan has probably never been
> higher than in the 1860s, nor his standard of living and
> access to education and travel... so satisfactory, nor the
> gap between him and the small, local manufacturers who
> employed him so narrow, nor that between him and the mass
> of labour so wide.[2]

In short, throughout the middle decades of the nineteenth century and
beyond, though probably never amounting to more than about 15 per cent
of the total working class, the labour aristocracy occupied a firm and
accepted position just below the employers, but very far above the
rest.[3] More or less comfortably ensconced in their ranks would be
found, it is arguable, the bulk of the first ships' engineers, those in
the larger vessels at any rate.

1   Royden Harrison, *Before the socialists* (Routledge & Kegan Paul, 1965)
     p.28.

2   Hobsbawm, 'Trends in the British labour movement', in his *Labouring
     men*, pp.316-43, p.324.

3   Hobsbawm, 'The labour aristocracy in nineteenth century Britain',
     in his *Labouring men*, p.296.

94

The preceding pages suggest that the first engineers to serve in the deep-water British mercantile marine would seem to have had little cause for complaint with their position on board ship, and that they possibly did not even perceive themselves to be engaged in a comparison with what they imagined to be the situation of others on board, in particular with the deck officers. And to the extent that they were with the deck officers so involved, it would seem unlikely from the engineers' point of view to have led to an assessment of comparative situations into which feelings of grievance and inequality would have obtruded to any degree. This is not to gainsay the possibility of an emerging sense of relative deprivation of status among certain ships' engineers vis-à-vis the executive on deck in particular cases: that is to say, the 'frequency' of relative deprivation, the proportion of the group who feel it, is of course variable, and only extensive research will establish, if it is to be done at all, the dimensions of this, and the degree of 'intensity' with which it was felt.[1] In sum, the suggestion has been that the first engineers to serve at sea occupied what we have described as a 'relatively privileged' position on board ship, which if not in relation to the deck officers was somewhat elevated to that of the lower orders, and more or less consistent with the extent of the engineers' contribution to the efficient performance of the vessel. A position too which was fortified by their superior earnings, a factor which thereby drew attention to the distinction in class and social standing ashore which their craft skills bestowed on them, and reflective similarly of their location in the shore-side class structure, 'just below the employers, but very far above the rest'. Such a position was not likely on the whole to have been productive of unfavourable comparisons and feelings of status deprivations between themselves and others on board. If such an interpretation is at all consonant with the reality of the position it might help to explain why that struggle for status within the shipboard hierarchy, which was to occupy a later generation of engineers than the one we have been considering, was in fact postponed until the later date.[2]

1   Runciman, 'Relative deprivation', pp.11-12.

2   See, Thomas W Fish, 'The status of engineers of the mercantile marine', *Transactions of the Institute of Marine Engineers*, V, No. XLVIII (1893-4) 5-22 ff.

APPENDIX

The rather familiar generalisation that people's attitudes, aspirations, failings, grievances, derive from and are largely inspired by the particular frame of reference within which they are conceived is, simply put, the informing principle of the related notions of relative deprivation and the reference group. The reference group chosen in any instance and the particular range of comparisons this selection induces or suggests will form the root of the relationship between inequality and grievance. In the discussion above it was suggested that the ships' engineers of the opening phase of mechanical propulsion at sea, insofar as they comprised a group at all, were a broadly homogeneous entity, one possessed of a comparatively limited frame of reference, content to identify with the outlook, position and prospects of the artisan class in engineering ashore, a series of qualified empirical generalizations which, in the context of an emerging labour force and a relatively archaic technology, might represent a tolerably fair estimate of the case. Space will not allow us to go into the question in detail here, but as time went on, consequent upon the developments in marine engineering technology, in naval architecture and in ship design, the greatly elaborating character of the work soon began to demand more from those intent on mastering it than mere solid self-discipline and sturdiness of purpose. In this context, the advent of the certificates of competency for engineers, in 1862, probably marked the first stage in the progressive closure of opportunities for the basically competent but untheoretical man and the sharpening of internal stratification in the occupation. For various reasons, for example the granting of certificates of service to those already in charge of a ship's engine-room allowing them to continue in this capacity, it would be some time before this trend would become clearly apparent, but in time the increasing size, output and complexity of the plant, its rising cost as a proportion of the total cost of the vessel, alongside the facts of tightening schedules, quicker turn-arounds, voyages of increasing length, would mean that a great deal more depended on the reliable operation of the vessel's machinery. Increasingly questions of insurance against its failure would tend to dominate, insurers' advice in the end dictating virtually the deployment and prospects of the labour force, those with certificates being in a position to improve their opportunities and rewards, those without being forced further away from the plum jobs. In essence, those engineers able and otherwise advantaged enough to seize the chances presented by the new technology were tending to pull away from the more practical minded toilers by hand, at the same time, it would appear, gaining cause to assess their social situation in terms of comparisons which it had not hitherto occurred to them to make. The more academically-inclined engineers, that is, seem to have been led to compare their new standing and growing influence with those in other occupations perceived by them to hold a position more in line with what they considered to be their own entitlement, this spiralling of aspirations generating a desire to rise, as it were, not so much with the membership group as out of it altogether. At the same time, a sense of relative deprivation of status seems to have been created where none existed before, on shipboard: i.e. an improving situation leading to a higher, not a lower, sense of relative deprivation.

In the following pages a series of passages from the transcript of a tape-recorded interview with a former ship's engineer, whose sea service ran from around 1904 to 1912, are presented, passages which touch on several of the points just considered. The interview was recorded as part of a project initiated in 1968 by the Director of the National Maritime Museum, Basil Greenhill, to collect the personal testimonies of men who had served at sea from the latter part of the last century until about the beginning of the Second World War. Oral history - the collection and use of what resides in the memory - ought not to be regarded as all that distinctive. It should be viewed simply as one approach among others in the work of the historian, permitting the investigator to obtain and employ testimony from a much wider group of sources than would otherwise be the case, sources consisting of individuals whose memories perhaps can be dredged for the sort of imaginative recounting of experience which, almost by definition, tends to be excluded from conventional documentary sources.

II

Our informant was born in Liverpool in 1881. The son of a chief engineer in the Cunard Line, he served his time in that company's repair shop in Liverpool from 1898 to 1904, and then served at sea, mainly in the ships of the same company, until 1912 or so, when he came ashore to take up an appointment in the Marine Survey Service of the Board of Trade. He considers first of all the position when he first started in the trade:

> The .... the thing was this .. there was very rapid changes taking place...the technical part of ships' machinery was making great strides and boiler pressures were going up, speeds were increasing, designs were greatly improved, and it came to a time when a much wider technical knowledge was required to take care of ships' plants. You must remember that the first men who went to sea were not seamen .. were not engineers, they were ... what we'd call ... millwrights, they were millwrights, and they were not welcome at sea at all, you see they were not seamen; and they had to fill the bill until the new type of engineer was evolved as this thing grew up...

> Well, I entered at a stage when this development had gone quite a long way - at the end of the century, and much larger engines, much higher powers and much more complicated machinery was coming into use: and a new type of engineer was required. It meant that they couldn't come from the bench, they had to go to a technical school, and learn a great deal more about the craft. Well that's how it came about that when I went to the engineering in 1898 I was immediately enrolled in a technical school, and I remained under instruction during the apprenticeship... but the point was this, the lads had to get up in the morning very early, they had to be at the shop at six in the morning, and there was no transport in those days, no buses you know, you had

to walk....then you were in the shop all day, on your feet until
5 o'clock, and you came home and had a meal, and three nights a
week, Mondays, Wednesdays and Fridays ... during the session you
had to be at the technical school, you had to walk there, and to
walk back and having got home - something after 10 - you had no
time for any frivolity, you had to be up by 5 ..... and I..I..I'd
six years of that, so there was no, not much room for any.. for
any loose living.

According to the informant, there were 22 apprentices in the shop in
those days and while all started evening classes in the autumn of each
year, as the session wore on:

... they dropped off bit by bit ... the dance schools, the dance
classes and other attractions wooed them up, so that by the time
the examinations came down the following May, only about 6 or 7
took the exam .....

Our informant, however, was made of sterner stuff and determined that
he was going to get on in the company, as his father had done before -
but his was a different aim:

..... the idea was that it was a very good company, in fact the
best company available, and he (father) said that I had got such
a good start that I would go far in the company. And at that
stage I was content with that. It was only when I'd been some
... 18 ... months an apprentice, that the vista began to lose
its brilliance and I began to contemplate a further development
which would give me a larger horizon .... My determination to
try and get this appointment (to the Board of Trade Marine
Survey Division), took place quite early in my apprenticeship ..
I remember the day, I remember the moment in fact; it was in
the early part of the year, probably in late March, I was going
down to the works, it was a sunny morning, bright sun, and I
was crossing the tram lines, and I was thinking of the monotony,
and deadness of the life - work to bed, and bed to work - and
the thought suddenly struck me that anyone who had a specific
objective was likely to make more progress, and more rapid
progress, because he had somewhere to go - he could direct all
his energies to one particular end. And it seemed so bright a
thought that I hung onto it, and I made up my mind what I'd
like to be - and the man that I thought was the great engineer
in my.. under my horizon, was the surveyor, who came to a ship
and he said this would do and this won't do and this would pass
and that wouldn't pass, and when you came to go to sea and get
your certificates he was the man who examined you, and I thought
he was a kind of demi-god! And I thought, I'll be one o' them
.. So that was what I went for; well I got there eventually ....

As he went on to point out:

Y'see, having joined a shipping company as a marine engineer
only a man who had made rather special preparatory ..... arrangements could hope to get out of it. Because, the position was
this, most men who found that they didn't like the life, they'd
probably happily married and the life was not congenial, and they

wanted to be at home - or maybe their wives were unsatisfied,
with their being away all the time, bringing up the family alone,
my mother had to bring up all her family without my father's
presence - so, it often happened that a man wanted to leave the
sea, but there was very little open to him except back to the
bench. Now and again they got odd jobs of one kind or another,
as agents for ships' supplies, packing and oil, and that sort of
thing; and when I told my father that I intended to leave the
company and endeavour to become a surveyor, he said, 'Well, you
know best and I wouldn't put out any difficulties in your way,
but I can only tell you this, in my experience I've known quite
a number of our men who've left the sea to better themselves, but
none o' them did it: they all finished up very badly off'.

> Didn't the chief's ticket itself, didn't it take you into
> better jobs ashore, away from the bench?

Oh yes, yes, you could get jobs, looking after somebody's plant
in a small firm...

> ...or in a power station, maybe, or that kind of thing?
> Was that about as far as you could get?

About as far as you could get, yes. And if you got an Extra
First Class Certificate, you could get into the boiler inspection,
the insurance business, and that was a life at home at any rate..
it was a pretty miserable existence, but it was a life at home.
... I had never any idea of remaining at sea. I had set my mind
on a career which required some years of experience at sea. But
it was a government appointment, and I had to do this sea service
to gain the experience and the qualifications before I could sit
for the examination ... That was why I went to sea.

Of the kinds of men who were still to be found serving at sea when he
first started, the following description was given:

They were all seniors, the senior men were all that type, and I
had two or three pretty good types to deal with in my time - they
really drank .... I remember one occasion, early in my career with
the company: there happened to be five large ships in port for
the annual overhaul, and there were so many engineers in port at
the time that they decided to have a get-together at one of the
Liverpool hotels. I don't know how many there would be, there
would probably be sixty of us turned up ... well we went to this
show and, ch...tch... it wasn't a show at all, t'was jist a binge.
The first thing was, we sat around at small tables in a large room
and the only equipment was whisky, two bottles on each table, and
glasses. Well, I didn't drink it at all, never touched it; but,
after a while, the engineer who was looking after the arrangement
...came round and said that the consumption had gone up and we
were in arrears and a whip-round would have to be made ... he
wanted 10 bob for each one. Well the juniors all paid up - but
I'll tell you what happened. The old men who drank the whisky,
when they saw two fellows with their heads together talking they'd

reach over from their own tables, put their hands over his
shoulder and take away his bottle of whisky. I saw that done
several times. The next thing was, one of them took the laces
out of his shoes, tied it round the bottle and the other end
round his wrist .... Ha! Heh! ... And that was in 1905 ....

As he pointed out, however, the old easy-going point of view was
being displaced by a new breed of engineer, a more thoughtful,
responsible kind of man altogether, and the recourse to the bottle
became a much rarer event.

Questioned about the strength of the deck/engine-room rivalry,
the following was elicited:

Oh! It was very marked ... On one occasion, when I was quite
new at sea, I was on night duty, one of the juniors had to stay
on night duty, at home, in port, one of the unmarried men, and
one of the mates. And the young mate and I were keeping the
ship in the evening, and he was talking to me, and he said,
'You know, I think there ought to be a regulation about our uni-
forms'. And I said, 'What's your idea?' He says, 'I think that
the executive', that was the deck department, '..should wear the
gold braid, and the engineers should wear silver braid'. I said,
'Do you think it's as marked as that, do you?' So he said, 'Well,
it would only be right, wouldn't it?' 'Well', I says, 'you can't
expect me to endorse a proposal of that kind. We're just as much
officers as you are, we have comparable responsibilities, and our
.... capability and qualifications take as much getting as yours
do. And we're not in any way inferior. You were here before us,
we know, we all know that, but that doesn't qualify you for a
superior status as officers of a, of the ship'. So, I wouldn't
agree with him.

What did he say to that?

Well, he hummed and hahed, he said he .. he thought the seniority
of the, the life at sea, the maritime life, entitled the seafarer,
the old-fashioned seafarer, to a little respect in view of his
long history. As I said, 'I know perfectly well the engineer's
an interloper. But the day is come when you simply can't do without him..' Hmhm?.......if you could do without him, you would...
but you can't....

Just in this context, how much of that...might have been
caused by the old style engineers?

A great deal! A great deal. You see, they resented the assumption,
the, not overt but covert, assumption of the deck crowd of their
superior status, and they were inclined to be a little belligerent
about it... and they put on their resentment rather obviously ....
and were inclined to be sharp about it.

But also here, these older men were a rough, in many ways,
maybe quite a coarse crowd, whereas the deck officers have
... come from, what you might say, nice, middle class backgrounds ...

.. Yes ..

> ... would that, do you think, have also aggravated it,
> the fact that they were just rough and tumble fitters,
> really?

Well, you see, they were, in the parlance of the day, the
'black squad' ... and, although they put on uniform occasionally, their normal clobber was a boiler suit: and that was
their status. And it went on like that ... for a long time.
But the times were changing very quickly and the technical
development in the machinery department was very rapid ... And
... I wrote a book when.. I left the sea...pointing out how
this disparity was very greatly in need of some care and
attention to dispose of it. And I wrote this book all about
the life at sea, and how, after a period of working together
they were seeing each other's point of view and finding how
much each depended on the other for the satisfactory discharge
of his responsibilities, that, the mutual cultivation of the
harmonious fellowship was a highly desirable idea ... And I
finished the ...a... book, with a fervent hope that the time
was not far distant when any kind of division between the two
departments would completely disappear and there would be one
body of sea-going officers .... Well, that day has now arrived,
and there is now an association of mercantile marine officers ...

> How much of this development was due to the fact that people
> like yourself were coming into the industry, you know,
> people with a more elaborate technical training ...

... it was the collective effect of people like myself, who
brought their personalities to bear on the problem; and it was
the effect on the deck department of finding that the men that
they were now going to have to deal with were men of practically
their own type and stamp; with their own point of view, their own
... type of mind, and .. thought, and character, and complete
fraternity was not....a difficult thing at all ... Especially,
when they were mutually helpful ...

III

The growing interest in oral history is a welcome development.
Oral history is capable not only of bringing the recent past more
excitingly to life but, by widening the range and scope of the available
evidence, is certain to inspire much new work and to lead to the re-
appraisal of assumptions about life in former times. As a former ship's
engineer I have always had a sort of latent regard for the subject of my
paper. But it was as much as anything the content of the interview reproduced above and of several like it with other engineers, which
awakened my interest in the whole question of the social history of
this neglected sector of the maritime labour force.

THE *MAGIC* : A WEST COUNTRY SCHOONER IN THE MEDITERRANEAN, 1833-9

David H Kennett

The Mediterranean has long been important in the maritime economy of
the South West of England.[1] From the sixteenth century onwards it
provided markets for pilchards caught in local waters and the cod taken
off Newfoundland. Tin and cloth were shipped out too from the South West
and in return a range of Mediterranean products, including wines, fruit
and oil,were brought back. By the early nineteenth century then these
trades were well-established and a notable part of the economy of the
South West. In that economy locally-owned shipping had a role, both as
carriers of commodities and as providers of employment, both direct and
indirect.

In this paper[2] we shall look at one vessel in the trade between the
South West and the Mediterranean in the 1830s. The *Magic* was a schooner
of 119 tons, jointly owned by three men, two of whom had Penzance
connections. She was newly built in 1833 and it would seem was sold in
1839. Between those years she made twelve voyages, the accounts of which
are preserved in one of the volumes which make up the Bolitho business
records now in the care of the Cornwall County Record Office, Truro, and
formerly in the library of the Royal Geological Society of Cornwall at
Penzance. The original I have not seen, but through the good offices of
the archivists at Truro, I was supplied with a complete copy of the
volume. There are in all fifty-eight pages of accounts relating to the

1   Discussion of the Mediterranean trade in earlier times is to be
     found in Ralph Davis, 'England and the Mediterranean, 1570-1670'
     in Frederick J Fisher, ed. *Essays in the economic and social
     history of Tudor and Stuart England* (Cambridge UP, 1961) pp.117-37,
     and thereafter in Ralph Davis, 'English foreign trade, 1660-1700'
     and 'English foreign trade, 1700-1774', in Walter E Minchinton, ed.
     *The growth of English overseas trade in the seventeenth and
     eighteenth centuries* (Methuen, 1969). Further discussion is
     provided by Ralph Davis, *The rise of the English shipping industry
     in the seventeenth and eighteenth centuries* (Macmillan, 1962,
     reprinted Newton Abbot: David & Charles, 1972), especially chap. XI,
     'The southern European and Mediterranean trades'. For a later
     period than the accounts of the *Magic* see Basil Greenhill, *The
     merchant schooners* (2 vols, Percival Marshall, 1951, 1957, reprinted
     Newton Abbot: David & Charles, 1968). Unfortunately Davis' comments
     stop at about 1780 and those of Greenhill do not begin until about
     1870.

2   I am indebted to the staff of the Cornwall County Record Office for

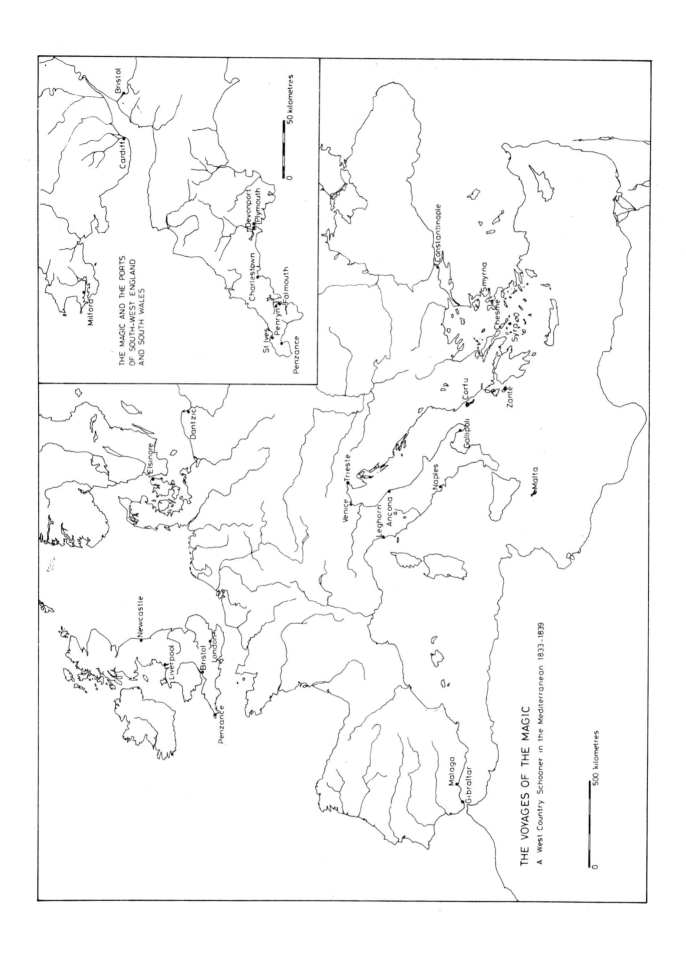

THE MAGIC AND THE PORTS
OF SOUTH-WEST ENGLAND
AND SOUTH WALES

50 kilometres

Bristol

Cardiff

Milford

Devonport
Plymouth

Charlestown

Falmouth
Penryn

St Ives

Penzance

Constantinople

Smyrna

Chesme

Syra

Corfu

Zante

Gallipoli

Malta

Dantzic

Elsinore

Newcastle

Liverpool

Bristol

London

Penzance

Venice

Trieste

Leghorn

Ancona

Naples

Malaga

Gibraltar

THE VOYAGES OF THE MAGIC

A West Country Schooner in the Mediterranean 1833-1839

500 kilometres

Magic, dating from August 1833 to 1 December 1839.[1] The actual volume was later used for the accounts of the master of the smack, *Chyandour,* Captain John Hair, with the vessel's owners, who may be presumed to have been Messrs Bolitho.[2]

The Bolithos were part owners of the *Magic.* Throughout its life, as recorded in the account book, they owned one half-share of the vessel. The remaining half was split equally between Joseph Carne and Captain Charles Trewavas, the latter for four and a half years being also master of the ship. Thomas and William Bolitho were prominent in the port of Penzance, described in 1830 as follows:[3]

> Few towns with reference to size are more flourishing. The trade of the port consists in exports of tin, in blocks, ingots and bars, to many foreign parts; and coastways in copper, tin, etc to London, Liverpool, Bristol and Wales; pilchards to the Mediterranean; and oil to Ireland. Its imports are tallow, hemp and iron from St Petersburg, and timber from Norway, Prussia and America; it receives coastways, iron and coal from Wales; corn and flour from Norfolk, Sussex, Hampshire and London; salt and bale-goods from Liverpool; groceries, bale-goods, and wine, spirits and porter by regular traders from London, Bristol and Plymouth.

Reference to the brief calendar of the Bolitho papers shows the brothers to have been involved in many of these trades, as does the list of the inhabitants of Penzance in 1830. Thomas and William Bolitho are reported as shipowners in the latter, but an exact knowledge of their precise holdings is not known to me. It would probably become apparent only from a careful study of all the Bolitho records.[4] At Chyandour, Thomas Bolitho

supplying me with a copy of the accounts of the *Magic.* Mrs C North, Senior Assistant Archivist, very kindly answered a number of queries and sent me a copy of the calendar of the Bolitho Business Records. For permission to publish these accounts of the *Magic* I wish to thank the Bolitho Estate Office and in particular Lt. Col. Sir E H W Bolitho.

1   Cornwall Record Office (CRO), Bolitho Business Records, Shipping Account Book 1833-50, D.D.RG 1/17.

2   I am not certain on this point: a quick examination by the Cornwall County Record Office did not reveal the name of the owners. The survival of the document in the Bolitho Business Records does though suggest a high degree of probability that they were the owners or part-owners.

3   This extract and all the subsequent extracts about Cornish and Welsh towns are taken from Pigot and Co, *London and provincial commercial directory and topography for 1830* (London and Manchester, 1830).

4   CRO Bolitho Records, D.D.RG 1/1- 1/183 and supplementary accessions unnumbered.

and Sons were recorded as tin smelters and most of the two hundred and fifty volumes which make up the Bolitho muniments refer directly to tin mining, over a long period. The earliest volumes date from 1703 and the latest continue to 1906, and cover a wide range of accounts, memoranda and miscellaneous matters for both tin mining and tin smelting in west Cornwall. The archive also includes three volumes of statistics of copper mining and twelve volumes concerned with the leather trade. Both at Penzance and at St Ives, Bolitho and Co were noted as fish curers and seine owners. While there is a single volume of fisheries accounts, 1824-1836, in the Bolitho papers,[1] this side of their business interests is more sparsely represented in the archive. However, a wide appreciation of the Bolitho business interests is given by the calendar of their papers, and to a certain extent this study is incomplete because these have not been used in detail. The records include three memorandum books, covering many aspects of the trading interests of the Bolithos, dating from 1814 to 1865, but mostly before 1837,[2] and examination of these, together with the fisheries accounts already noted, would doubtless throw considerable light on the relationship of the *Magic* to their general business interests.

The two other owners of the vessel have been more difficult to track down, both being less prominent in the business life of west Cornwall. Joseph Carne was a Penzance ship owner and tin merchant,[3] related no doubt to William and Edward Carne, ship owners of Market Street, Plymouth. Joseph Carne appears in the Bolitho papers as a tin merchant and on occasion used the *Magic* to export his own tin. Of the third member of the partnership, Charles Trewavas, little can be said. Owner of a quarter of the vessel and master for the first nine voyages, he is not recorded as a ship owner or ship master in any town in Cornwall in 1830. For the tenth and subsequent voyages, his son, Richard Trewavas, was master of the vessel, having served as the mate on the eighth voyage and probably also on the ninth voyage.

As stated above the account book of the *Magic* covers the period from August 1833 to December 1839.[4] The first three and a half months

1   CRO Newlyn and St Ives Fisheries Accounts, 1824-36, D.D.RG 1/4. This also contains timber and other sundry accounts.

2   CRO Memorandum Book, 1814-33; Memorandum Book, 1817-28; Memorandum Book, 1816-35, with pilchard statistics, 1845-65; respectively D.D.RG 1/74, 1/75 and 1/76.

3   Personal details for both Carne and the Bolithos are derived from Pigot, *Commercial directory* (1830). There is no extant copy of a directory issued by the firm of Pigot between 1831 and 1844 which covers Cornwall.

4   Details given below and not individually noticed are derived from the account book, CRO D.D.RG 1/17.

refer to the accounts of first cost and outfit from Bristol, summarised on 10 November 1833. Thereafter she had a trading life of six years. Throughout the life of the account book, the accounts were written in a consistent, clerkish hand which would suggest that they were made up after each voyage. They are purely running accounts, and several items are omitted. There is, for instance, no mention of insurance of the vessel though primage on the various freights carried is recorded. Later in the paper reference will be made to this topic, but at this point it may be noted that there is no attempt at a dividend on the capital invested. Rather profits were more likely calculated as a simple excess of income over the running expenses of the ship. Another deficiency is that no record survives of her value when she was sold.

The six years of the ship's life as recorded by the account book cover twelve different voyages. Each is from an English (or Welsh) port returning to an English port. I have dealt with each voyage as such. Excepting two, the seventh and the ninth, each was a voyage to the Mediterranean, mostly to ports in the eastern Mediterranean.

II

The first three pages of the accounts of the *Magic* refer to the initial costs of the vessel, bought in Bristol from Messrs Tucker, who on 8 November 1833 were paid £1170. This is the major part of the expenses of the first cost and outfit, totalling £1867 2s 3d. Tuckers also presented a second bill of £12 14s 0d on the same day as the 'account for purchase'. The remaining bills of these three and a half months are smaller, but they include three of over a hundred pounds and one of nearly this sum:

12 Oct.	Williams and Foster, for copper	£110	18s 4d
1 Nov.	Haramans account	£126	1s 8d
7 Nov.	Cook, Thatcher & Co for rope	£105	6s 11d
8 Nov.	W D Matthews, sailmaker, corrected and sent back to him	£87	6s 8d

The substance of the second of these is not known. Other, smaller, accounts reflect the lesser costs of fitting out a schooner in the 1830s. Accoutrements for the ship included rigging leather, 18s 2d; carpenter's tools, nails etc, £3 4s 6d; a medicine box, £1 11s 0d; plumber's work by James Ruggs, £5 9s 3d; cotton tarpaulins and sail coverings from J C Watts, £18 0s 6d; and bills for sails and blocks. A sailmaker from Hayle, Cornwall, Harvey & Co, supplied sails to the value of £24 16s 7d. Two blockmakers supplied tackle: Thomas Cook whose bill was £23 12s 0d and Cox who charged £7 17s 5d. Three sizeable accounts were paid on 8 November:

King and Sons for Compasses, Glass and Telescopes	£6	0s 0d
John's, Blacksmith's Account	£32	7s 0d
Read, painter's bills	£7	3s 0d

Two further sizeable items in the expenditure were the costs of transport between Hayle and Bristol, a total of £8 18s 0d, for journies both by land and by sea in August and September 1833, and for wages and board in Bristol, a total of £31 10s 8d.

In sum, £1867 2s 3d was spent in Bristol before the vessel had earned a single penny for her owners. To this was added the 'Ship's Stock', held by the master, £94 17s 9d. The latter remained a feature of the accounts until the vessel ceased to be recorded.

III

The *Magic* cleared Bristol on 12 November 1833 with 12 tons of tin in her hold for Cardiff. There she loaded iron for Syra and after visiting both Milford Haven and Penzance on the outward voyage began her career as a west country schooner trading to the eastern Mediterranean. The voyages, listed in Appendix 1, covered twelve ports in the six years. Some were visited only once: Ancona, Leghorn, Naples and Gallipoli. Others were more frequent ports of call. The *Magic* called at Smyrna five times, and Syra three times. Constantinople, Venice, Corfu and Zante were each visited twice. She only made two voyages outside of the Mediterranean: the seventh to the Baltic and the ninth round Britain. The latter, from Newcastle to Liverpool, seems essentially to have been a voyage of convenience though cargo was carried on each of the separate legs, with calls at Devonport and Charlestown.

This was a steady, but not especially spectacular, career, though probably not untypical of vessels of her kind. Comparative instances are difficult to document, but two may be noted. The *Bertha*, under Captain Matthew Mitchell, made six voyages to the same area between 1845 and 1849. Constantinople was the destination three times, Odessa twice and Smyrna and Beirut once each. This vessel was ultimately lost in the North Atlantic, making a passage home from Virginia.[1]
The brigantine, the *Kara*, of Cardiff, had a known working life between 1838 and 1844. After bringing coffee on a return voyage from Haiti, she seems to have been employed in the Mediterranean trade, with Palermo and Messina in Sicily apparently frequent ports of call. She also visited Naples and Leghorn, as well as Smyrna, before being wrecked somewhere near Nantes, whilst carrying coals from Newcastle.[2]

1   Michael Bouquet, *South eastern sail* (Newton Abbot: David & Charles, 1972) p.108.

2   Peter Mathias and Alan W H Pearsall, *Shipping: a survey of historical records* (Newton Abbot: David & Charles, 1971) p.113, gives some details of the extensive papers relating to this vessel. Others have kindly been supplied to me by Mrs P Moore, County Archivist for Glamorgan. Their study would make an interesting comparison with the *Magic*.

Both these vessels show a familiarity with certain ports and a custom and routine demonstrated by constant trading in the same area for a number of years.

The *Magic* has this same routine, governed largely by the outward cargo, listed in Appendix 2 for each voyage, rather than by any purely Mediterranean considerations. Among these cargoes three items are prominent: iron, tin and pilchards. The two last, it will be noted, were among the various business interests of the Bolitho family, and it is here that additional work on the papers in Truro would provide useful further information.

Each of the four voyages with pilchards as the main cargo began in St Ives, where according to Pigot in 1830:

> The pilchard fishery is carried on to a greater extent than upon any other part of the coast of Cornwall, and in some seasons there are nearly one hundred seines in requisition in the town. The season commences in July and continues till the latter end of November, during which in prolific seasons some 3500 hogsheads are taken, each hogshead containing about 2000 fish, which are cured here and chiefly sent to Italian markets.[1]

The four cargoes of pilchards carried by the *Magic* varied between 614 and 650 hogsheads and can each be construed as a minimum of a sixth of the total pilchard catch of the town, on this evidence. That, if true, may give some indication of the economic standing of the Bolitho family.[2]

The Bolithos were also tin merchants, and on her voyages to Ancona and Leghorn with pilchards the *Magic* carried a small quantity of tin, two tons in both cases. On the twelfth, and last recorded, voyage, the route was more complex and the cargo manifest more split up. Part of the cargo from Plymouth to Cardiff was 13½ tons of tin. The cargo from Britain to Constantinople included three separate consignments of tin. Four tons in twenty barrels were for Mr Carne, presumably Joseph Carne, one of the owners of the *Magic*. The other two consignments, one of 38 tons in 190 barrels, the other of two tons in 10 barrels, were not specified as to their owners, but one may suspect the Bolitho interests as such.

1   For further details of St Ives, see Richard Pearse, *The ports and harbours of Cornwall* (St. Austell: Warne, 1963) pp.107-16, especially 112-13.

2   Further on the Bolithos, Cyril Noall, *A history of Cornish mail and stage coaches* (Truro: Bradford Barton, 1963) has a description of their Cornish house. And Robert S Craig, 'Shipowning in the south-west in its national context, 1800-1914', in Harold E S Fisher and Walter E Minchinton, eds. *Transport and shipowning in the westcountry* (University of Exeter, 1973) p.40, records a schooner, the *Camilla* of 114 tons, built in 1825 for the Bolithos, and sold to Edward Hain in 1838.

If this is so, the freight rates, recorded for all identifiable cargoes and which are given in Appendix 4, may not represent the true economic rates, because of cargoes owned by the vessel's shareholders. This may very well be true of the small quantities of tin carried on the eighth and eleventh voyages. An apparent discrepancy in any case is here recorded for the freight rates for tin on these two voyages, because it takes rather longer to sail to Ancona than it does to Leghorn: an outward voyage in these cases of 69 days as opposed to 46 days. This seems to be reinforced by the rates charged for the pilchards: as one would expect significantly more on the Ancona voyage than on the Leghorn one.

To answer the interesting issue just raised of normal freight rates and those for owners would need further work on the Bolitho muniments. Tin when carried might well have been mostly a cargo owned by the Bolithos, but iron from Cardiff would seem not to have been their property. On the last voyage, the twelfth, 112 tons of iron and tin plates were carried from Cardiff, where, as Pigot stated in 1830 there was 'a good harbour from which great quantities of wrought iron, tin, coal, glass bottles, etc are exported'. The *Magic* had earlier earned freight from Cardiff iron, in December 1833 to Syra and in August 1835 to Syra and Smyrna. In each of these three cases the same freight rate was charged.

As to homeward freights, a variety of cargoes was secured in Smyrna, frequently after a cargo had been delivered elsewhere. Only once, and then with only a part cargo, was Smyrna the direct destination of the outward journey. Valonia, the acorn cups of the valonia oak, used in tanning and dyeing, were carried on the first and twelfth voyages. Alone of the inward cargoes, this would seem to have a connection with the Bolitho interests, for their account books include several which refer to leather working.[1] However, the destination of the first return voyage was Liverpool, not Penzance. Raisins were the cargo on the fourth voyage, when the *Magic* docked in London; similarly currants were carried from Zante to Newcastle on the eighth voyage. These seem to reflect what could be obtained as a return cargo, as do the cargoes of oil. Oil was brought from Corfu to London on the third voyage and to the same port from Gallipoli on the Gulf of Tarranto on the tenth voyage. Though each of these traditional products of the eastern Mediterranean, long shipped to England, may have been a cargo obtained there, rather than a contracted cargo specified by an importer, there can be no doubt that they were profitable to the ship. The *Magic's* earnings on nearly all her voyages (see Appendix 9 for details of earnings) owed significantly more to the inward cargo from the Mediterranean than to those taken out.

Only one substantial cargo seems to have been secured in the same Mediterranean port as was the destination port on the outward journey.

1   Particularly CRO D.D.RG 1/5 - 1/14 and 1/80 - 1/81. These cover 1819 to 1881.

This was in early March 1839, when 674½ quarters of wheat were shipped at Leghorn for Plymouth - it might be added at twice the earnings of the pilchards and tin cargoes which were carried outwards. Wheat was also the cargo on the sole north European voyage, when an unspecified amount of grain was shipped from Meluish[1]to London in September 1837.

This sole excursion into northern waters was not at all a well-producing venture, there apparently being only a light shipment out (see Appendices 2 and 9). One voyage only, the ninth, was recorded in British coastal waters in toto, but other voyages, as they have been here defined, included a period carrying a cargo from one British port to another (Appendix 3). The ninth voyage, from Newcastle to Liverpool, took coal to Devonport, limestone to Charlestown, and china clay from Charlestown to Liverpool. On other voyages in British waters the cargoes were less noticeable as money earners for the *Magic* (Appendix 9), but their revenue did help to augment the ship's income.

Between Mediterranean ports the *Magic* was usually in ballast, as between Ancona and Zante in January 1838 and between Naples and Gallipoli in September 1838. However, one cargo was secured in the Mediterranean. A quantity of boxwood was carried from Constantinople to Smyrna in July-August 1839.

The victualling records show that a crew of seven, the master, mate, four seamen and a boy, seem to have been the usual ship's complement. For much of the ship's life, one of the seamen was paid five shillings per month extra, suggesting he was an A.B. rather than an O.S. For instance, on the Dantzic/Elsinore voyage of July-October 1837, S Kemp, G R Squire and H Walker were paid at the rate of £2 5s 0d per month, but James Busben received £2 10s 0d each month (more wage data is given below). Most voyages seem to have had one or more members from the previous voyage, as shown in Appendix 8, which lists those who spent more than one single voyage on the *Magic*. W George is typical of those whose association with the vessel was not short-lived. He seems to have joined in Milford Haven on the return leg of the fifth voyage and then remained on board to sail to Venice in the following year. For four months of the sixth voyage he assumed extra responsibilities and was paid five shillings more per month. On the last two voyages, five members, including the master, served both to sail to Leghorn and then to Constantinople and Smyrna. It can be noted also that one of them was paid off for two weeks between the two voyages, but the seaman, Wood, obviously either could not find another vessel or was prepared to wait until the *Magic* sailed again. The consistency of crew membership does suggest that the *Magic* was not an unhappy ship for these six years of its life. Apart from the master and the mate the crew had five other members. With twelve voyages, this gives sixty places to be filled in the fo'c'le in these years. A third were filled by men who had stayed on for another voyage.

1   Presumably Melhus in Norway, near Trondheim.

IV

On any voyage, victualling costs and the wages of the crew were a significant proportion of the outgoings. The evidence for this has been summarised in Appendix 7. The proportion varied from a high of 60 per cent on the eighth voyage to a low of 19 per cent on the seventh voyage. However, this latter voyage entailed extensive repairs in London and corrected figures of percentages on the usual operating costs for this and the fifth voyage are given in Appendix 7A. This makes the comparisons with other voyages more valid, since although large repair bills were paid on these voyages, their cause, the general wear and tear of the sea, can be said to have arisen from all the previous voyages. Using the corrected figures, the total percentage for both victualling and wages varied between 35 per cent and 60 per cent with a median of 47 per cent and a mean of 47 per cent. Victualling costs varied between 11 per cent and 22 per cent, a median of 16 per cent and a mean also of 16 per cent. Wages on the other hand accounted for between 18 per cent and 38 per cent, with the median of 28 per cent slightly below the mean of 29 per cent. It is noticeable that the voyages with the fewest days are those with the lowest percentages both for wages and for victualling.

Victualling costs were charged at thirteen pence per man, except for the last voyage when fourteen pence per day per man was allowed. All wage rates were on a monthly basis, though often a man was paid for x months and y days, as on the eighth voyage when Richard Trewavas, mate, was paid for 5 months and 22 days. His father, Charles Trewavas, when master was paid £7 per month, but the son when he commanded received only £6 monthly. Richard Trewavas as mate had been paid £3 10s 0d monthly, but more usually the mate was paid £3 3s 0d. On the second and third voyages he was paid £3 10s 0d, perhaps suggesting the same man as on the first voyage. It seems evident, however, that the mate, usually unnamed, was recruited for the voyage and paid off at the end of it. On the seventh voyage to Dantzic and Elsinore, he was paid only £2 15s 0d. An able seaman paid £2 10s 0d was also carried on this voyage, as well as the three seamen who were paid a monthly wage of £2 5s 0d. These were the rates from the third voyage, but on the second voyage the ordinary seamen were paid £2 2s 0d monthly. On the initial voyage a variety of rates were offered, between thirty shillings and fifty shillings. No two men who served for any length of time on this voyage appear to have been paid the same amount. The ship also carried a boy, who was clearly paid according to his experience. A Watkins was remunerated at £1 5s 0d on the second voyage, but on the third voyage his monthly wages were £2 0s 0d. T Gelio, when he joined in Gallipoli on the tenth voyage, was paid £1 0s 0d per month. Later he received £1 10s 0d. J Devaux began at £1 5s 0d, but after his first voyage, the sixth, received £2 0s 0d per month. It may be that though still a juvenile he was capable of a seaman's work. Often it was the boy who remained on the ship while she was in port.

V

While wages and victuals were the prime outgoings, the schooner did incur other expenses on each voyage. To facilitate discussion of these, three voyages have been chosen for detailed examination: the fourth, the fifth and the eighth. These reflect respectively the iron trade, the use of the vessel for general trading, and the pilchard trade. Items from other voyages can then be related to these where appropriate for an examination of the expenses incurred in running a schooner in the 1830s.

The accounts of the fourth voyage begin in London on 17 July 1835; they end in London on 16 January 1836. Total expenses on the voyage were £365 0s 6d; those excepting victuals and wages amounted to £173 0s 1d. What may be called the non-recurrent expenses of the voyage were incurred in London, Penzance, Cardiff, Syra, Smyrna, Gibraltar and London.

In London in July 1835, stores cost £9 9s 4d, with an extra bill of £1 8s 7d, both from R Jolly. Canvas to the value of £8 2s 0d was also bought. The only other major item at this time was ballast:

40 tons Trinity ballast	£2 10s 0d
Heavy ballast	£1 0s 6d
30 waggons ballast at Greenhithe	£1 12s 6d

Connected with this presumably were waterman's expenses of £1 6s 6d and another 10s 0d at Greenhithe. Candles were also purchased in London and shop articles. A sailor, T Cook, a member of neither the preceding nor the succeeding crew, spent a week working on board and was paid 16s 11d. At Penzance minor expenses only were incurred, including 19s 0d for medicine. Rather more was spent in Cardiff, where the *Magic* loaded iron for the Mediterranean. The largest bill was from a shipwright, Friduin, for £3 10s 5d, but there was also 19s 10d for blacksmith's work, from John Richards, and assorted nails were purchased, costing 11s 11d. Three tons of coals were bought, £1 4s 0d, and paints and oil came to £1 2s 3d. The remaining expenses incurred were those of being in port:

Canal dues on 119 tons at 2d per ton	19s	10d
Custom House clearance, lights etc	£1 14s	6d
Pilotage in and out, 157 tons iron at 2d per ton	£1 6s	2d
Boat hire sundry times in the canal	2s	6d

Also incurred were costs of stowage:

Stevedores, 158 tons iron at 2d per ton	£1 6s	2d
1 labourer stowing 150 tons at 1d	12s	6d

These slightly varying cargo bases for the calculation of costs may be noted: the full size of the iron cargo, as recorded at the final destination, was 158 tons 2 cwt 2 qtr 1 lb.

Abroad the expenses on this fourth voyage were no less heavy. At Syra, a small island in the Cyclades which seems to have attracted importance as an entrepôt for the iron trade, there is only one recorded account: pilotage and lighterage, £4 4s 6d. When the *Magic* had earlier called at Syra, in March 1834 on the first voyage, more substantial expenses were incurred:

	£	s	d
Waterman's account	7	10	2
Consul's account	1	10	2
Assistance at sea		8	8
Commission at 3 per cent	5	16	7
Primage on the freight	4	17	3
Allowances in discharging the cargo	1	0	0

They total £21 2s 10d. At Syra on the second voyage, later in 1834, when the port expenses are recorded in local currency, they came to £1 13s 0d and were only consul's and port charges and an agent's account. Clearly expenses on different voyages in the same port could show wide variation. To return to the fourth voyage, at Smyrna two accounts, both in local currency, were made up. The first, for £18 10s 5d, covered commission, brokerage, consul's charges and postages; the second, amounting to £14 2s 9d, comprised a ship's chandler's bill with an additional expense for a boat tending the ship, an account of a supplier at Chesme, where a bill of health was also levied, and remuneration for assistance in mending sails. On her return voyage to England, the *Magic* called briefly at Gibraltar, where port charges of £3 10s 8d were levied. On the arrival of the *Magic* in London in January 1836, further expenses were still to come. Two pilots and a waterman cost £20 5s 7d, and there were expenses relating to the inward cargo of £29 1s 0d. The master's primage on the freight was £9 0s 6d. Also noted at this point was six months spirits and wine for the cabin, and grog, £6 0s 0d.

The *Magic* returned to London on 8 January 1836. She remained in port until 24 April. During this time expenses of £151 16s 6d were incurred. The largest bill was for stores and sails from Richard Jolly, £63 15s 0d, with an additional bill of £1 0s 11d. Considerable repairs seem to have been done in these three and a half months. There are payments to riggers, 4s 9d; to joiners, £1 3s 3½d; for paint and lead, 10s 6d; to a blacksmith, 19s 5d; to a mast maker, £2 19s 0d; and Richard Hayward and Sons presented an undetailed account for £9 8s 6d. More than one sailor was employed and provisioned during this time, as was a boy, Leonard Munn, who served on board for 55 days. Candles and coals, obviously for consumption in port, were a recurrent expense. One final item, 12s 6d for the repair of a brass blunderbuss, may serve to remind us that trade was not always without the possibility of incident. In preparation for the coming voyage, the fifth, a stock of coals was also purchased, £1 16s 6d, from Thompson. Those for port use were small in cost: 1s 4d and 1s 2d was spent in January. When the cargo was stowed, the stevedores cost £5 0s 0d, and there was an account of £5 2s 6d for dock rent and water supplies. An account for port charges in all totalled

£23 13s 6d, but this included brokerage on the freight of £9 3s 0d, lights outward of £4 10s 6d, and entering and clearing out £3 3s 0d. The other major expense within the London charges of 1836 was pilotage, £9 0s 4d, but two shillings should be added to this for steamer fare for the master.

The fifth voyage was to Corfu, Zante and Smyrna, delivering cargo at the first two, securing a return cargo at the third. At Corfu, expenses totalled £24 1s 7½d. An agent, Charltens, was used and a detailed bill presented in English rather than local currency. It includes items regularly found, such as port and health charges, £1 10s 6d, and commission on the freight, £4 7s 1¼d, and other less common items. These included 42 tons ballast at 20 pence per ton and a caulker's bill of £6 12s 6d. Repairs done abroad, however, seem only to have been the necessary; all large-scale repair work was done in England. Labourers to discharge the lighters were paid 18s 0d at Corfu, and those working on board, £1 3s 9d. At Zante a similar range of costs was encountered - port and health charges, labourers and ballast; but an unusual item was gunpowder. At Smyrna, the charges were levied in Turkish currency, and a total presented in sterling. This was £22 4s 4d and included costs of stores, caulking, unloading the ballast, a boat and two hands to fetch water, a pair of ash oars and commission.

The return voyage from Smyrna to Milford, between 18 July and 10 October 1836, was made without calling at a port in the western Mediterranean. In Milford a total of £58 10s 8½d was spent. Over half relates to a shipwright's bill, from William Roberts, £18 11s 5d, and a sailmaker's bill of £14 6s 0d from William Browning. An account for stores came to £9 13s 4d. Also spent in Milford was money on rope junk, 19s 0d; paint, 7s 0d; tallow, 1s 4½d; and a block, 1s 9d. Part of the cargo was discharged: expenses here included allowances for discharging and stowing the wool, £2 0s 0d; stevedore, £1 4s 6d; victualling of the stevedore for eight days, 8s 8d; and sundry expenses of a lighter crew and a guard ship, £1 8s 0d. The last were not victualled. Release charges at the Custom House were £1 4s 6d, and lights and clearance, £2 6s 6d. Finally to clear the harbour, there was the pilot, who cost 15s 0d.

The *Magic* then sailed for Liverpool, partly in ballast: in Milford, £1 15s 0d had been spent on 20 tons of stone. At Liverpool, the regular costs of a vessel entering port were:

	£	s	d
Dock dues at 1s 7½d per ton	9	13	4
Lights	2	19	6
Pilotage, 9ft 6in at 9s per foot	4	5	6
Anchorage postages		5	0
Brokerage on the freight at 2 per cent	7	16	4

Beyond this expenditure of £24 19s 8d, there were few expenses. £2 0s 0d was to Edward Welch, lump discharging cargo, and the remainder, in all £1 12s 9d, was divided between the salvage of a buoy, 5s 0d, and the same for boat and hands, 7s 0d each for deck lights and a time glass

and lamp, 3s 9d for padlocks, and another 5s Od for stages and planks.
One final item remains of the voyage's costs: ten months grog for the
crew and extras for the cabin, £10 Os Od. The cost of this was a
pound per month throughout the sea-going life of the ship.

The *Magic* sailed from Liverpool in early December 1836. At
St Ives, she loaded fish for Venice, and on her return made her Baltic
voyage. The costs of these two voyages, the sixth and the seventh, are
not considered in detail. The eighth voyage of October 1837 to April
1838 to Ancona and Zante, with Cornish pilchards, will now be considered.

In October 1837, the *Magic* had returned from Dantzic with a cargo
of grain which was discharged at London. Here she underwent extensive
repairs:

	£	s	d
Smith and Harpur, shipwright's bill	80	10	5
Glascote Brothers, balance for copper	91	7	5
Remuneration to smack's crew	36	0	0
Tug steamer to Commercial Dock	4	0	0
Ditto to Rottenburey's Dock	1	0	0
Sundry men pumping day and night	3	15	0
Men scraping the ship throughout	1	0	0

No details survive of these large bills, in all totalling £217 12s 10d.
The accounts for repairs were counted within the seventh voyage and
covered its loss. For the eighth voyage, few items were recorded in
London and an account was made up on 17 October 1837. Forty tons of
Trinity ballast and a smaller (unspecified) amount of heavy ballast
were bought and a waterman's services were recompensed. At Gravesend
a new boom was purchased for £5 8s Od.

From the Downs, apparently reached without a pilot, the schooner
sailed to Penzance. Here a total of £8 19s 3d was spent. Harbour dues
were £1 13s 5d, the charges at the Custom House were £1 10s 3d and the
pilot in and out, with expenses, was recorded at 17s Od. The remainder
was an interesting but essentially minor group of small charges: the
largest being 30 cwts of coals, £1 10s Od. A few minor repairs were
done: a smith and a brazier charged 5s 9d and 7s 3d respectively. A
map cost 2s 4d, a padlock and corkscrew 3s 8d, a chisel 1s 3d, and
2s 10d was spent on candles. Ballast carriers were purchased for
17s Od and medicine for 12s 3d. The English accounts frequently include
candles and medicine.

At St Ives the costs again were small: £18 16s 9d in all. Three
major items made up most of this bill: pilotage and loading, £5 13s Od;
carriage, ballast and water, £3 18s 4d; and ship requisites, rope and a
sailmaker, totalling £6 8s 3d. Nails and a crow bar were also bought as
was a gallon of lamp oil. The last is an unusual item in these accounts.

On this voyage, two Mediterranean ports were visited: Ancona, where
the *Magic* was not known, Zante where she had been before. In Ancona,

most of the £30 17s 6d which was spent was taken up by a bill from Mr Acquabonans. That was for £22 14s 0d, and no details are given. The master's primage on the freight was £6 15s 6d and allowances for discharging the cargo and loading ballast were £1 0s 0d. Harbour dues at Celphalonia were 8s 0d. In Zante, about the same total was spent, £28 7s 2½d being recorded. Three main items were noted: disbursements from Woodleys, £9 11s 6½d; the stevedores' account, £9 7s 1d; and Lawrence and Hays' commission, £8 1s 8d. Allowances to the stevedores and crew were noted at £1 0s 0d, and there were three small items: a kettle, 2s 0d, lard 3s 4d, and postage, 1s 4d.

The next port of call was Falmouth, where there is an account of 31 March 1838. The Zante account is noted at 7 February and that for Ancona at 3 January. In Falmouth, the largest item was pilotage in and out, £3 10s 0d, from a total of £7 6s 4½d. A shipwright's bill came to £2 1s 0d, and £1 0s 0d was spent on expenses going to Penzance. The other items were small: harbour dues of 2s 6d; tar at 6s 7½d; a log book 2s 6d, and candles 3s 9½d. The voyage ended in Newcastle where the account is dated 21 April 1838. Pilotage up the river was charged at 17s 0d, and there is a cryptic item of 'noting protest 5s 0d', not it might be added for the first time. Commission on the freight in Newcastle was accounted at £7 17s 6d, and master's primage on the freight at the same. Lights, Ramsgate and Dover duty were noted at £6 17s 6d, and the bar pilot at 13s 9d. A pound was allowed for discharging and a shilling spent on a mooring ring.

The *Magic* sailed out of Newcastle within the week. She had only eighteen months of her recorded life left. There were three more voyages to the Mediterranean. At the end of the twelfth voyage she finally came home to Penzance. Here a bill for sails of £33 2s 6d was reimbursed to Captain Trewavas, the son. It was the largest item in the final accounts. The *Magic* had sailed home for the last time.

VI

The question remains, as Professor Davis posed it in 1962: was it a profitable business?[1]

There are many ways of answering the question. The first cost and outfit of the *Magic* came to £1867 2s 3d. The total profit on the six years was just under this sum, at £1757 16s 4½d. But that excludes the resale value of the *Magic,* which is not known to me. That lack of information means that we cannot assume that the overall profits on the period for which the accounts have survived represent a loss of five

1   Ralph Davis, *English shipping industry*, pp.363, 387.

per cent on the capital invested. Even the equation when balanced by
the addition of the (unknown) value of the *Magic* in 1839 is perhaps a
sophisticated modern concept which probably did not enter the minds
of the owners. This is not to say they were not interested in profit,
but rather that they looked at the profits made in a different light
to this. It is more probable that the profit, being the excess of
income over expenditure, if calculated in percentage terms was calculated as a percentage of the income. Even this may be too abstruse
a definition. In all probability, the profit was seen in terms purely
of the excess of income over expenditure. They made no allowance for
depreciation and there is no record of insurance costs.

In this, the most probable contemporary, light the *Magic* made
considerable profits. Three voyages only (see Appendix 5) made a loss:
the fifth, the seventh and the ninth. On the fifth voyage the loss was
£54 2s 4½d. In the accounts, £151 16s 6d was spent in London during an
inactive three months. A ship is not earning money lying idle in port.
Inactivity and also repairs may explain this loss on the running
accounts. No cargo was taken out on the seventh voyage and £217 12s 10d
was spent on repairs in London. The loss on the voyage was £218 8s 5d.
These two are almost equivalent sums. The ninth voyage was one of convenience and the loss small, only £8 19s 9d.

If we return to the second of these three losing voyages, the
seventh, to the Baltic, we see that the return earnings almost covered
the loss. On the nine profitable voyages it was the return cargo which
earned the greater proportion of the income, often strikingly so.
Appendix 9 records the differences on earnings from inward and outward
cargoes. It is rare to find, as on the third voyage, almost equivalent
sums. It is frequent to find very substantial differences. We have
noted that the owners of the *Magic* included Thomas and William Bolitho,
tin merchants and fish curers. The fish and the tin shipped in the
vessel could both have been their property, and the rate charged consequently not the economic one, but rather a lower rate or one charged
as sufficient to be earned to sail the ship and its cargo to Italy or
the Turkish empire. The return cargoes brought in large sums, more than
four hundred pounds on three of the voyages. Appendix 9 suggests the
owners expected the greater proportion of the earnings to come from the
homeward journey. That cargoes were always secured, despite some movement to other ports, suggests there was never expected to be other than
a minimal delay in finding another cargo.

Putting the question of profit on one side we may note the great
variety of social good a ship could do. It provided work for a large
number of men. They included not merely those obviously benefiting, the
sailors; nor even the perhaps equally obvious men in shore-based ship
industries, such as chandlers and shipwrights, caulkers and coppersmiths.
For beyond this there was the employment created by the use in the *Magic*
and the hundreds of small vessels like her of ship's accoutrements and
their manufacture, often many miles from the ports. In any discussion
of the place of shipping in the national economy, or even in the local
economy, it is as well to remember men such as those who made marline

spikes in Birmingham or who twisted rope in Penzance. These implications for employment and income, together with the possibility that the Bolithos used the vessel for their own purposes, as it is specifically recorded they did on the last voyage, should make an examination of the idea of profitability broader and perhaps more enlightening.

But the *Magic* did make considerable profits, simply in terms of income over running costs. Appendix 5 shows the profits made and Appendix 6 their division. Only in the period from 17 July 1837 to 24 June 1838 was it not possible to pay out a goodly sum. One may consider that the owners were rather more than satisfied.

The profits were divided, one half to Thomas and William Bolitho, and one quarter each to Joseph Carne and Charles Trewavas. For the Bolithos, the *Magic* was a worthwhile investment. They had the income from her earnings, they had a carrier for their tin and their pilchards. When no outward freight was available in St Ives or Penzance, other freight could be and was sought, in Cardiff, in Liverpool and in London. Joseph Carne also used the vessel for his tin: on the twelfth voyage, twenty barrels, being four tons, of tin were carried for him. This Penzance tin merchant could thus also receive the preferential freight rates as an owner and have also the profits of a supplementary investment. For Charles Trewavas, there was not merely a quarter share in the profits of running the ship, but the income he received between 1833 and 1838 as master, with which went the primage on the freight and half the value of the cabin freight. It was he who perhaps benefited most from the initial investment.

VII

In November 1839 the *Magic* unloaded her last cargo, at Penryn and at Penzance. Her accounts were then closed, the ship's stock returned to the accounts, and the profits totalled. We may assume the ship was then sold. Her subsequent history is unknown, but perhaps after six years and twelve voyages her owners considered she had come to the end of her useful life as a vessel engaged in the Mediterranean trades.

APPENDIX 1

The voyages of the *Magic* : dates, ports of call

(M - Mediterranean)

Voyage	Dates	Ports
1 (M)	12 Nov. 1833- 6 July 1834	Bristol, Cardiff, Milford Haven, Penzance, Syra, Smyrna, Liverpool
2 (M)	7 July- 21 Dec. 1834	Liverpool, Syra, Constantinople, Smyrna, Chesme, London
3 (M)	22 Dec. 1834- 16 July 1835	London, Ramsgate, Penzance, St Ives, Venice, Trieste, Zante, Corfu, Malta, Falmouth, London
4 (M)	17 July 1835- 16 Jan. 1836	London, Penzance, Cardiff, Syra, Smyrna, Gibraltar, London
5 (M)	17 Jan. 1836- 25 Nov. 1836	London, Corfu, Zante, Smyrna, Milford Haven, Liverpool
6 (M)	26 Nov. 1836- 16 July 1837	Liverpool, St Ives, Venice, Malaga, London
7	17 July- 10 Oct. 1837	London, Dantzic, Elsinore, London
8 (M)	11 Oct. 1837- 25 Apr. 1838	London, Penzance, St Ives, Ancona, Zante, Falmouth, Newcastle
9	22 Apr.- 24 June 1838	Newcastle, Devonport, Charlestown, Liverpool
10 (M)	25 June- 14 Dec. 1838	Liverpool, Naples, Gallipoli, Falmouth, Plymouth, London
11 (M)	15 Dec. 1838- 7 Apr. 1839	London, Falmouth, Penzance, St Ives, Leghorn, Gibraltar, Plymouth
12 (M)	11 Apr.- 12 Nov. 1839	Plymouth, Penzance, Cardiff, Penzance, Constantinople, Smyrna, Gibraltar, Penryn, Penzance

APPENDIX 2

Cargoes carried on the *Magic*, 1833-1839 : long distance voyages

Voyage	Cargo outwards	Cargo inwards
1 (M)	Cardiff - Syra: 57¾ tons iron	Smyrna - Liverpool: 124 tons 7 cwt 20 lb valonia 16 tons 1 cwt 2 qtr 26 lb emery Yellow binces (cabin freight)
2 (M)	Liverpool - Constantinople: Lump freight	Smyrna - London: not specified
3 (M)	St Ives - Venice: 650 hogsheads pilchards	Corfu - London: about 90 tons oil Cabin passengers
4 (M)	Cardiff - Syra: 59 tons 16 cwt 2 qtr 10 lb iron Cardiff - Smyrna: 98 tons 5 cwt 3 qtr 19 lb iron	Smyrna and Chesme - London: 127 tons 18 cwt 1 qtr raisins
5 (M)	London - Corfu and Zante: not specified Female passenger and child	Smyrna - Milford Haven: Lump freight with wool and skins
6 (M)	St Ives - Venice: 650 hogsheads pilchards	Venice - London: General cargo
7	London - Baltic: In ballast; but the *Magic* carried firewood and a parcel	Meluish - London: Grain
8 (M)	St Ives - Ancona: 614 hogsheads pilchards 2 tons tin	Zante - Newcastle: 109 tons 2 cwt 2 qtr 8 lb currants
9	English waters (see Appendix 3)	
10 (M)	Liverpool - Naples Measurement goods	Gallipoli - London: 178 casks oil (25449 gallons)
11 (M)	Penzance and St Ives - Leghorn: 642 hogsheads pilchards 2 tons tin	Leghorn - Plymouth: 674½ qtrs wheat
12 (M)	Cardiff - Constantinople: 112 tons iron and tin plates Penzance - Constantinople: 44 tons tin	Constantinople - Smyrna: Boxwood Smyrna - Falmouth and Penzance: 114 tons 17 cwt valonia Opium and otto roses (cabin freight)

APPENDIX 3

Cargoes of the *Magic*, 1833 - 1839 : in British waters

Voyage	Ports	Cargo
1 (M)	Bristol - Cardiff	12 tons tin
6 (M)	Liverpool - St Ives	Salt and coals
8 (M)	London - Penzance	47¾ tons extract
9	Newcastle - Devonport	7½ keels coal
	Devonport - Charlestown	Limestone
	Charlestown - Liverpool	172 tons clay - three separate cargoes
12 (M)	Plymouth - Cardiff	13½ tons tin
	Penzance - Cardiff	Limestone

APPENDIX 4

Freight rates for selected commodities

Voyage		Commodity	Voyage	Rate
1	(M)	Iron	Cardiff-Syra	22s 6d per ton
4	(M)	Iron	Cardiff-Syra	22s 6d per ton
4	(M)	Iron	Cardiff-Smyrna	22s 6d per ton
12	(M)	Iron and tin plates	Cardiff-Constantinople	20s 0d per ton
3	(M)	Pilchards	St Ives-Venice	8s 0d per hogshead
6	(M)	Pilchards	St Ives-Venice	8s 6d per hogshead
8	(M)	Pilchards	St Ives-Ancona	8s 0d per hogshead
11	(M)	Pilchards	St Ives-Leghorn	6s 0d per hogshead
1		Tin	Bristol-Cardiff	2s 0d per ton
8	(M)	Tin	St Ives-Ancona	15s 0d per ton
12		Tin	Plymouth-Cardiff	8s 6d per ton
12	(M)	Tin	Penzance-Constantinople	25s 0d per ton
11	(M)	Tin	St Ives-Leghorn	20s 0d per ton
1	(M)	Valonia	Smyrna-Liverpool	52s 0d per ton
12	(M)	Valonia	Smyrna-Falmouth	70s 0d per ton
3	(M)	Oil	Corfu-London	55s 0d per ton
10	(M)	Oil	Gallipoli-London	60s 0d per ton
4	(M)	Raisins	Smyrna-London	52s 6d per ton
8	(M)	Currants	Zante-Newcastle	52s 6d per ton
11	(M)	Wheat	Leghorn-Plymouth	11s 0d per qtr
9		China clay	Charlestown-Liverpool	8s 3d per ton
9		Coal	Newcastle-Devonport	£17 1s per keel

APPENDIX 5

The *Magic*, 1833-1839 : income, expenditure and profits

Voyage		Income			Expenditure			Profits			Notes
		£	s	d	£	s	d	£	s	d	
1	(M)	556	7	10	409	1	2	147	6	8	
2	(M)	681	2	2	367	10	2	313	12	0	
3	(M)	574	5	2	453	18	8	120	6	5	
4	(M)	563	6	8	365	0	6	198	6	2	
5	(M)	601	4	3	655	6	7½	Loss: £54 2s 4½d			London expenses of £151 16s 6d
6	(M)	739	4	2	538	14	4	200	9	10	
7		213	3	9	431	12	2	Loss: £218 8s 5d			Repairs at London: £217 12s 10d
8	(M)	613	3	5	351	16	5	261	6	11	
9		211	0	6	220	0	3	Loss: £8 19s 9d			Voyage round coast of Britain
10	(M)	601	8	5	369	9	11	231	18	6	
11	(M)	633	18	10	350	12	8	283	6	2	
12	(M)	807	3	11	511	19	0	295	4	11	

APPENDIX 6

The *Magic*, 1833-1839 : the division of the profits

Voyage		Total profit to be divided			Bolitho			Carne and Trewavas			Notes
		£	s	d	£	s	d	£	s	d	
1	(M)	147	6	8	73	16	4	36	16	8	
2	(M)	313	12	O	156	16	O	78	8	O	
3	(M)	120	6	5	60	3	2½	30	1	7¼	
4	(M)	198	6	2	99	3	1	49	11	O½	
5	(M)										Loss on voyage of £54 2s 4½d
6	(M)	146	7	5	73	3	9	36	11	10	Total profit of sixth voyage was £200 9s 10d
7											Loss on voyage of £218 8s 5d
8	(M)										Total profit of eighth voyage was £261 6s 11d
9											Loss on voyage of £8 19s 9½d
7 - 9		21	13	1½	10	16	7	5	8	3	Division of the small profits of the three voyages
10	(M)	231	18	6	100	O	O	50	O	O	£31 18s 6d retained by Bolitho
11	(M)	314	19	8	125	O	O	62	10	O	£64 19s 8d retained by Bolitho
12	(M)	295	4	11	147	12	5	73	16	3	End of Account

APPENDIX 7

The *Magic*, 1833-1839 : operating costs, victuals and wages

Voyage	Total expenditure (a)			Days	Victuals (b)			(b) as % of (a)	Wages (c)			(c) as % of (a)
	£	s	d		£	s	d		£	s	d	
1 (M)	409	1	2	226	89	3	2	22	152	13	8	37
2 (M)	367	10	2	168/ 147	59	10	7	16	107	7	9	29
3 (M)	453	18	8	198	77	3	9	17	146	15	4	32
4 (M)	365	0	6	177	69	2	4	19	122	18	1	34
5 (M)	655	6	7½	310	87	19	4	13	172	2	7	26
6 (M)	538	14	4	227/ 207	88	5	2	16	148	6	0	27
7	431	12	2	96	29	15	0	7	53	7	6	12
8 (M)	351	16	5	193	78	2	2	22	134	16	4	38
9	220	0	3	64	23	19	6	11	42	9	8	18
10 (M)	369	9	11	133	60	1	5	16	101	17	11	29
11 (M)	350	12	8	117/ 92	44	7	3	13	78	2	2	22
12 (M)	511	19	0	231/ 216	91	14	0	18	147	4	0	29

APPENDIX 7A

The *Magic*, 1833-1839 : operating costs, victuals and wages
on voyages with major repair bills

Voyage	Expenditure less repair costs (a)			Days	Victuals (b)			(b) as % of (a)	Wages (c)			(c) as % of (a)
	£	s	d		£	s	d		£	s	d	
5 (M)	503	10	1½	201	87	19	4	17	172	2	7	34
7	213	19	4	58	29	15	10	14	53	7	6	25

APPENDIX 8

The *Magic*, 1833-1839 : crew stability

Name	Voyages	Total days
A Watkins	2, 3	375
D Oliver	2, 3, 4	545
T Burkett	3, 4	372
R Hogg	5, 6	435
W George	part 5, 6	234
J Devaux	6, 7, 8, 9, part 10	619
G Rey	part 8, 9	150
T Hodge	part 9, 10	150
T Gelio	part 10, 11, 12	409
- Rodgers	11, 12	329
- Wood	11, 12	316
- Vaughan	11, 12	329

APPENDIX 9

The *Magic*, 1833-1839 : analysis of earnings

Voyage	Outward journey			Inward journey			Coastal trade			Total		
	£	s	d	£	s	d	£	s	d	£	s	d
1 (M)	194	9	5	339	10	10	1	4	0	556	7	10
2 (M)	230	0	0	451	2	2				681	2	2
3 (M)	286	0	0	278	0	7				574	5	1
4 (M)	201	6	6	362	0	2				563	6	8
5 (M)	191	2	4	300	0	0				601	4	3
6 (M)	297	9	6	326	7	0	20	9	11	739	4	2
7	2	6	0	192	8	3				213	3	9
8 (M)	271	16	2	315	2	3	24	7	6	613	3	5
9							214	0	6	214	0	6
10 (M)	245	8	8	344	4	3				601	8	5
11 (M)	214	1	2	418	11	6				633	18	10
12 (M)	178	2	0	422	1	5	13	17	9	644	8	0
							21	10	0			

Notes

1 Minor items and cabin freights are omitted throughout this table.

2 In voyages 5 and 6 the master's stock of £94 17s 9d is included in the total in the document.

3 The second figure for coastal trade in voyage 12 represents earnings in the Mediterranean.

THE *BATTEN CASTLE* : THE ACCOUNT BOOK OF A SMALL
HOME-TRADE SAILING VESSEL, 1852-66

Richard Pearse

The *Batten Castle* was built at Plymouth in 1851 by William Routleff.
She was a small sailing vessel of 62 register tons (57 63/100 tons when
remeasured in 1859 under the Merchant Shipping Act of 1854); she was
carvel built with framework and planking of wood. She had a single mast
and was rigged as a sloop. Her measurements were : length 57 5/10 feet,
breadth 17 3/10 feet, and depth 8 feet. Her carrying capacity was about
95 tons of bulk cargo.

William Routleff did not live long after building the vessel. In
April 1852 his executors sold her to Charles Couch, described as a shipowner of Plymouth. By 1 May - within one week - Couch had transferred
32 of his 64 shares of 1/64th each to eight people, including four
shares each to six members of the Routleff family, all of them domiciled
at Plymstock, now a suburb of Plymouth. By 1858 Charles Couch had disposed
of half of his remaining 32 shares. The other shareholders now included
only one Routleff - Joseph - a shipwright of Plymstock. Theophilus Couch,
son of Charles, had become the principal shareholder with 28 shares. He
was a master mariner of Port Isaac in Cornwall, and was to be the master
of the *Batten Castle* throughout her career until she was lost in the
Bristol Channel in September 1866 - that is one year under William
Routleff's ownership, and 14 years and 5 months under the management of
Charles Couch.

The *Batten Castle* belonged to that numerically very large category
of small coasters that found employment in the British coastal trades in
the middle decades of the nineteenth century. The survival of her
account book for the years 1852-66 enables us to look closely at the
business done by one West Country vessel and to make some observations
about her income, running costs and profitability.

The account book on which this paper is based[1] contains 152 voyage
accounts for the period from 1 May 1852 to 17 September 1866. The book
is an unbroken record voyage by voyage of the ship's earnings from
freight and of her operating expenses. The volume itself is a large

---

1   The account book is in the possession of Mrs H Couch of Ty-Mor,
     Pentewan, Cornwall. Mrs Couch is the widow of Mr Charles Couch,
     ship-broker of St Austell, who died some ten years ago at the
     age of 80, and who was the grandson of Theophilus Couch, master
     and part-owner of the *Batten Castle*. No other papers or books
     relating to the vessel appear to have survived. I am most
     grateful to Mrs Couch for kindly permitting me to study this
     record.

standard type of ledger with ruled columns, and it is in such good condition after being in use for more than 14 years that one can only assume that it was not taken to sea, but kept ashore. It is clear that voyage accounts were not infrequently written up well after the completion of a voyage; in a few cases after two or three voyages. With the exception of a spell of 14 voyages in 1863-4 the handwriting is the same throughout, that of the master, Theophilus Couch.

There were two methods of paying the ship's disbursements. First, payments in coin were made on the spot wherever the ship happened to be at the time. These ready cash payments state specifically what the money was spent on : such items as harbour, towage and pilotage dues; sundry supplies such as coal for the galley, lamp oil, candles, paint, brooms, planks etc; minor running repairs; some loading and discharging costs; and of course wages and the victualling allowance of the master and his crew of three. All these details throw much light on coastal shipping routines and customs, and also hint at some of the hazards and hardships endured by the crew.

Secondly, the majority of the voyage accounts include one or more items shown as 'bills paid'. These give only the amounts paid and the names of the firms or people to whom they were paid, and do not disclose the nature of the expenditure covered by the bills. The recipients of these monies, who allowed the ship's owners to run a credit account, are in many cases identifiable as ship-brokers, ship-chandlers, sailmakers, ship-builders and repairers, carpenters and so on. It is not possible to analyse accurately these expenses under 'bills paid'; they could relate to a refit, overhauling, replacements, major repairs, or in some cases to labour costs in loading or discharging cargo, or commissions etc incurred by brokers on the master's behalf.

The *Batten Castle* traded mainly, in one direction, between the Clyde and south-west England, that is from Glasgow to Plymouth, and in the other direction from Pentewan to Glasgow. There were also some intermediate voyages to and from South Wales, to Cornish ports other than Pentewan, to London, to a few ports along the coast from Exeter to Portsmouth, and to Rouen.

During her career the vessel rounded the Land's End 145 times, an average of 10 times a year. She was evidently built to stand up to the severe buffetings she had to endure in the Irish Sea, which in stormy weather is the most turbulent area of water around our coasts. In the 14 years and 5 months she was under Couch management the *Batten Castle* made 255 calls at 44 different ports to load or discharge cargo, including ballast cargoes. Table 1 lists the frequency of calls.

Despite competition from the expanding network of railways and from steam-powered vessels there was much carrying business for small sailing coasters in the growing national economy. They had the advantage of flexibility in that they could go where they chose, to isolated places and into shallow creeks and waters, whereas goods

Table 1

Clyde ports	67
Ardrossan	2
General Irish Sea area and South Wales	33
Pentewan	47
Other Cornish ports	22
Plymouth	47
Morwellham (on the Tamar above Plymouth)	8
Other south coast ports	18
London	4
Newcastle-on-Tyne	1
Rouen	6
	255

trains were confined to fixed railway tracks.

It is evident from the account book that the *Batten Castle* used Mevagissey as her home port. She called there 17 times without ever loading or discharging a cargo. This port is only two miles from Pentewan where she called 47 times to load cargo. Three of the ship's four larger suppliers were domiciled at Mevagissey: the firms of Lelean (shipbuilders), Furse (sailmakers) and Pearse (rope-makers, coopers and ship-owners). The fourth was Shapcott, sailmakers of Plymouth. Mevagissey, more easily accessible than Pentewan, was also far better equipped with repair, maintenance and victualling facilities. The vessel certainly did not call there under stress of bad weather, as she apparently did on many occasions at other ports. Shelter could be found in the immediate vicinity at Fowey at a cost of only 1/4d in harbour dues, whereas Mevagissey cost £1 a time in pilotage and harbour dues. The following table shows the number of unscheduled calls at 19 ports without discharging or loading cargo. In many, but not in all cases, the vessel must have been seeking shelter from unfavourable weather.

Table 2

Carlingford	1	Penzance	6
Coombe (? Combe Martin)	1	Plymouth	1
		Polkerris (near Par)	1
Dartmouth	1	Ramsgate	2
Dover	2	Rothesay	1
Fowey	8	St Ives	2
Holyhead	3	St Mawes	5
Howth (near Dublin)	1	Strangford (northern Ireland)	6
Ilfracombe	3		
Milford	5	Weymouth	1
Padstow	11		
			61

Throughout her career the *Batten Castle* maintained the same general pattern of trading, carrying three main types of cargo:

1 China clay, ball clay and china stone from south-west England to the Clyde.

2 Iron products and mixed general cargoes, including unspecified cargoes, to south-west England and the south coast.

3 Mixed general cargoes to South Wales, and coal from South Wales mainly to Cornwall and Devon.

There were 97 cargoes of raw materials, 72 cargoes of general merchandise including processed iron products, and three cargoes of primary food products. The complete range of cargoes, together with their frequency, and the freights earned on each type of product, is shown in Table 3.

With one or two exceptions the cargoes of clay and china stone were almost certainly delivered to the firm now much enlarged and known under the title Armitage/Shanks, sanitary ware manufacturers of Barrhead, near Glasgow. More than half the 28 cargoes described in the account book as iron, pig iron and iron castings, were delivered to Plymouth (including Devonport and Saltash) and Morwellham. It is a Couch family tradition that one of their ships brought iron products from somewhere in the north to Plymouth for use in the construction of Brunel's railway bridge across the Tamar (the bridge was opened to traffic in 1859). Cargoes of iron products also went to other south coast ports and to the only foreign port figuring in the vessel's voyages, Rouen.

All the copper ore cargoes were shipped from Morwellham to South Wales for refining. The freights earned on this traffic were ridiculously low - from 3/- to 4/- a ton. Five of the six limestone cargoes also earned very low freights. In 1862 a cargo of 80 tons from Drogheda to Glasgow earned only 2/- a ton. The same absurdly low rate of freight was earned on a cargo of 75 tons from Plymouth to Glasgow. This was in 1863. In this period, 1862-3, china clay freights were also at their lowest; the owners must have been temporarily hard put for cargoes to have been compelled to accept such unrewarding freights.

Amongst the less frequent cargoes there was a consignment of scrap iron sent from Southampton to Greenock at the comparatively good total freight of £45. The solitary cargo of salt was shipped from Liverpool to Langston on the south coast; and the only cargo of Portland stone was discharged at Millbay Dock, Plymouth, although there was no shortage of good low-priced building stone in the immediate Plymouth area. Of the four cargoes of sand, one was shipped from Topsham to Plymouth; another from Plymouth to Newcastle (the *Batten Castle's* only voyage in the North Sea north of the Thames estuary); one from Yarmouth in the Isle of Wight to Bristol, and one from Belfast to Glasgow. In three cases the freights on this very common commodity were no higher than those received for the cargoes of copper ore and limestone, the highest being 4/- a ton.

Table 3

Nature of cargo	Raw materials				General and manufactured goods			
	No. of cargoes	Freight earned			No. of cargoes	Freight earned		
		£	s	d		£	s	d
China clay	42	1,254	6	5				
China stone	8	281	4	9				
Ball clay	4	113	19	3				
Iron					10½	471	9	8
Pig iron					12	696	5	11
Iron castings					5½	347	7	11
Scrap iron	1	45	0	0				
Coal (15), Culm (1)	16	557	5	11				
Copper ore	8	122	0	0				
Limestone	6	68	12	4				
General cargo and cargo not specified (but including iron products and whisky)					41	2,529	12	0
Sand	4	79	9	10				
Iron ore	2	18	5	8				
Bricks					2	85	6	2
Manure	3	67	17	0				
Salt	1	50	5	4				
Machinery					1	75	0	0
Portland stone	1	17	0	0				
Illegible (? Valonia)	1	32	10	0				
	97	£2,707	16	6	72	£4,205	1	8
Primary food products:								
Wheat					1	21	10	0
Potatoes					1	40	19	0
Flour					1	46	15	0
					75	£4,314	5	8

Total freight earned:					Average per cargo		
Raw materials	97	£2,707	16	6	..... £27	18s	4d
General and manufactured goods	72	£4,205	1	8)			
Primary food products	3	109	4	0)	..... £57	10s	6d
	172	£7,022	2	2			

The sand shipped from Plymouth to Newcastle may have been of an unusual nature for a special use, the freight being relatively high at 10/- a ton. Of the three cargoes of manure, all shipped from Plymouth, two went to Ireland and one to Pentewan. Two cargoes of bricks were shipped from Bridgwater, one to London and the other to Plymouth. The vessel carried only three cargoes of primary foodstuffs : potatoes from Rouen to London, wheat from London to Bristol and flour from Rouen to Liverpool.

The contents and composition of the most profitable cargoes - general and unspecified merchandise out of Glasgow - are not disclosed, although in some cases mention is made of whisky and iron castings as part cargoes. The high freights earned on these cargoes indicate that the commodities were of high value, and were certainly not raw materials. In no case is the tonnage shown, possibly because the master saw no point in listing various miscellaneous crated and packaged goods in his account book. The entry in every case is limited to something like this : 'Freight on general cargo £ x '.

Although the account book contains 152 voyage accounts the vessel made 218 separate voyages between two single ports with cargo of one kind or another : 172 cargoes earning freight, and 46 ballast cargoes. The difference arises from the system of writing up the voyage accounts sometimes weeks or even months later. In all cases the master treated as only one voyage a freight-earning cargo as well as the preceding or following ballast cargo. In nine cases he telescoped three voyages into one, and in one unusual case he wrote up two freight-earning cargoes and two ballast voyages as a single voyage. We thus have 67 voyages that are not recorded separately from an accounting point of view. It is therefore impossible to analyse individual voyage costs with any exactitude. One has to work on averages.

On the many short ballast voyages from Plymouth to Pentewan the ship carried from 40 to 50 tons of ballast in tubs, equivalent in weight to half a normal cargo, incurring labour costs and a second lot of pilotage and harbour dues, as well as wages and victuals for the crew. Such ballast voyages brought no compensating reward, as they earned no freight. The *Batten Castle* was fortunate in that she had to make only half a dozen ballast voyages of any great distance : Pentewan to South Wales was the longest.

From the figures in Table 3 above we can examine the profitability of the two main categories of cargo - raw materials and general merchandise.

The 97 cargoes of raw materials brought in £2,707 16s 6d
   (or an average of £27 18s 4d per cargo)

The 75 cargoes of iron products, general
   merchandise or manufactured goods, and
   food products brought in a total of £4,314 5s 8d
   (or an average of £57 10s 6d per cargo)
                                                   ─────────────────
                                                   £7,022 2s 2d

Overall between 1852 and 1866 there was, if anything, a fractional fall in the value of freights, in daily wage and victualling costs, and (most markedly) in harbour and dock dues. The following figures show how freights varied on the more frequent types of cargo between the earlier and later years of the ship's trading:

Of the 54 cargoes of clays and china stone the first 10 averaged 6/9d per ton, and the last 10 averaged 6/5d per ton. Seasonal variations between summer and winter were: lowest 5/6d, highest 8/6d.

Of the 16 cargoes of coal the first 6 averaged 7/9d per ton, and the last 6 7/6d per ton. Seasonal variations between summer and winter were: lowest 5/6d, highest 10/3d.

Of the 41 cargoes of general and unspecified merchandise the first 10 earned a total of £671 15s 11d, an average of £67 3s 7d, and the last 10 earned a total of £643 13s 9d, an average of £64 7s 5d per cargo.

Turning now to disbursements we find that more than half the total i.e. £3,362 2s 3d out of £6,318 10s 3d, represents the cost of manning the vessel - wages and the victualling allowance for the crew of four, comprising the master, mate, man and boy. There was no increase after 1854 in the basic rates, although there were frequent minor fluctuations in wages up and down due to changes involving replacement of crew members. Table 4 shows the daily cost of wages and victualling taken from one voyage account beginning in the June of each year. The daily rate of the same order, within a few pence, runs through all the voyage accounts for each year.

Table 4

	s	d		s	d
1852	11	0	1859	13	2
1853	12	0	1860	13	2
1854	13	8	1861	13	6
1855	14	6*	1862	13	2
1856	13	11	1863	13	8
1857	13	8	1864	13	6
1858	13	0	1865	13	2
			1866	13	2

* Increase due to a man replacing the boy for several months after the latter was drowned on a voyage to Glasgow.

Of the remaining expenditure of £2,956 just over £450 was paid to the Mevagissey and Plymouth firms engaged in the job of keeping the vessel in good repair, including the supplying of a new main mast, a top mast, new sails and other essential equipment.

It is not possible to determine how much of the remaining sum of £2,506 should be apportioned to each of the remaining main categories of expenditure. The cost of 'moving' the ship about : pilotage, towage, river and harbour dues, 'assistance' etc was not small, varying from about £3 10s 0d to about £10 per voyage, depending on the ports visited. Apart from Rouen, Glasgow was the most expensive port, although the cost of going up and down the Clyde and of harbour dues fell in the ship's later years. The first six calls cost an average of £8 5s 0d a call, whilst the last six visits worked out at an average of £6 13s 0d a visit. The other regular ports of call - Plymouth and Pentewan - were not expensive, but here again the cost was slightly lower in the later years than in the earlier.

Unfavourable weather was expensive for the *Batten Castle*, and sent up the cost of operating the ship. Harbour and towage dues had to be paid at most of the ports to which the vessel had to run for shelter, but still more expensive were the wages and victualling allowance paid to the master and his crew for the many days, and sometimes weeks, spent sheltering from bad weather. Table 2 above shows that the vessel made 61 unscheduled calls, many of which must have been under stress of weather. Many of the ship's voyages were exceptionally slow. Taking into account not only delays due to bad weather, but waiting time at ports for the loading and discharging of cargo, no less than 84 of the 152 freight-earning voyages each took 30 days or more in terms of wages and victuals. One voyage lasted 94 days, and 14 others more than 50 days each. We shall return to the significance of this point later.

The remaining category of disbursements - commissions, small running repairs, sundry supplies such as brooms, planks, baskets, coal for the galley, candles, paint and very often additional labour for handling cargo - were continually incurred, and added up to another sizeable proportion of the total cost of operating the ship.

II

We shall now turn to the question of the ship's profitability. Table 5 divides the *Batten Castle's* career into two approximate halves in terms of the number of voyages performed. There were 88 voyages in the first 'half' of 6 years and 8 months, but only 84 voyages in the longer second 'half' of 7 years 9 months.

It will be seen that the first 88 voyages brought in an apparent operating profit altogether of £560 13s 11d, and the last 84 voyages only £142 18s 0d. The total apparent profit of £703 11s 11d is almost exactly 10 per cent of the total freights earned.

We have seen that neither the rate of freight earnings nor that of disbursements increased, rather, if anything, marginally decreasing during the ship's life. The reasons for the poorer profitability in the

Table 5

| Year | DISBURSEMENTS | | | Freight earned | Apparent annual profit (loss) | No. of freight-earning voyages | No. of days on which wages and victuals paid | Average duration of voyages |
	Wages and victuals	Other expenses	Total					
	£ s d	£ s d	£ s d	£ s d	£ s d			
1852	150 11 3	108 3 11	258 15 2	302 5 10	43 10 8	10	274	
1853	204 11 9	244 17 0	449 8 9	522 8 7	72 19 10	15	337	
1854	246 6 11	315 2 11	561 9 10	742 7 1	180 17 3	16	361	
1855	239 8 10	176 7 7	415 16 5	498 19 3	83 2 10	10	328	
1856	240 17 10	262 16 8	503 14 6	545 12 6	41 18 0	13	334	
1857	258 9 0	212 4 5	470 13 5	600 0 6	129 7 1	15	374[1]	
1858	215 17 9	170 4 0	386 1 9	395 0 0	8 18 3	9	302	
	1,556 3 4	1,489 16 6	3,045 19 10	3,606 13 9	560 13 11	88	2,310	= 26.3 days per voyage
1859	231 11 4	249 10 11	481 2 3	480 17 3	(- 5 0)	12	376[12]	
1860	235 18 2	209 9 2	445 7 4	469 18 0	241 10 8	11	390[13]	
1861	191 16 6	166 3 3	357 19 9	382 15 3	24 15 6	8	291	
1862	261 7 4	201 6 11	462 14 3	472 18 2	10 3 11	12	395[1]	
1863	238 16 1	211 7 1	450 3 2	491 5 9	41 2 7	12	355	
1864	269 5 2	164 0 4	433 5 6	507 9 9	74 4 3	10	391[1]	
1865	245 14 6	169 19 11	415 14 5	400 3 2	(15 11 3)	11	362[1]	
1866	131 9 10	94 13 11	226 3 9	210 1 1	(16 2 8)	8	202	
	1,805 18 11	1,466 11 6	3,272 10 5	3,415 8 5	142 18 0	84	2,762	= 32.9 days per voyage
TOTALS	3,362 2 3	2,956 8 0	6,318 10 3	7,022 2 2	703 11 11	172	5,072	

Notes

1 In these years voyages beginning in mid or late December lasted well into the succeeding year.
2 Master's wages and victuals 376 days; rest of crew 358 days.
3 Master's wages and victuals 390 days; rest of crew 321 days.

second period of 7 years and 9 months must be sought elsewhere. The figures in the last two columns of Table 5 provide the answer. The first 88 voyages occupied 2,310 days on which wages and victualling allowance and other running expenses were paid, giving an average of 26.3 days per voyage. The last 84 voyages occupied 2,762 days, giving an average duration of 32.9 days per voyage. In neither period were the full wages and victualling allowance paid while the ship was laid up at Mevagissey for overhaul or major replacements. Of the first 88 voyages 35, or well under half, lasted 30 days or longer, but only 5 of them more than 50 days. Of the last 84 voyages 49, or well over half, lasted 30 days or longer, and 11 of them more than 50 days.

The vessel thus cost far more to operate, despite almost identical rates of earnings and expenditure, in the second period, 1859-66, than in the first, 1852-8. The two periods are further compared in Table 6 below. Whilst average income per voyage remained constant, the average expenditure per voyage rose in the second period, owing to the longer time taken on average over the 84 voyages. Why the period from 1859-66 should have been marked by longer voyage times on average and hence lower profitability is not at all clear.

Table 6

Period	No. of Voyages	Freight earned			Average freight per voyage			Disburse- ments			Average disbursement per voyage			Average profit per voyage		
		£	s	d	£	s	d	£	s	d	£	s	d	£	s	d
1852-8 (6 yrs 8 mths)	88	3606	13	9	40	19	9	3045	19	10	34	12	3	6	7	6
1859-66 (7 yrs 9 mths)	84	3415	8	5	40	13	2	3272	10	5	38	19	2	1	14	0

Thus we have 88 voyages x £6 7s 6d profit £561
and 84 voyages x £1 14s 0d profit £142
_____
£703

This sum of £703 is only the apparent profit since the account book excludes the charges for insurance and for depreciation of capital invested. Taken together these charges would probably more than swallow up the £703. There is evidence in the account book that the insurance premiums payable to the clubs at Padstow and Topsham were taken care of by Charles Couch outside the account book. A separate note inserted in the book reports that for a period of 25 months the insurance premium averaged £1 9s 0d per month. Over the full period of 14 years and 9 months the premium, if at the same rate, would have reached £247. But if the account book excludes insurance premiums it also takes no account of the amount recovered from the insurance clubs after the vessel was lost at sea in 1866.

THE RISE OF ILFRACOMBE AS A SEASIDE RESORT

IN THE NINETEENTH AND EARLY TWENTIETH CENTURIES

Bruce May

Leisure and tourism are relatively new fields of historical study, but in the twentieth century their growing economic and social import- ance both nationally and regionally, have brought them greater recognition. The development of leisure is, in many ways, as revealing of emergent industrial society in nineteenth century Britain as the world of work upon which most historians' efforts have hitherto con- centrated. This study traces the development up to 1914 of Ilfracombe, the foremost holiday resort in North Devon - an area virtually unknown to outsiders until its emergence as a leisure centre attracting in its heyday before the Great War visitors from several of the royal families of Europe. At its peak Ilfracombe drew hundreds of thousands of visitors each year, and by the 1900s was fancifully considered by the popular press as a potential threat to Blackpool and Scarborough. Numerous factors, both external and internal, shaped this development. In part it was the product of the rising demand for leisure which urban- industrial expansion fostered in an increasingly wide social sector, and the shifting pattern of holiday-makers' expectations from the passive experience of relaxation and recuperation at the sea-shore to more active and organised pursuits. It was also governed by local factors, part- icularly the ability and willingness of the community to respond to this demand and capitalise on the area's natural attractions. In a brief survey it is not possible to examine every aspect of Ilfracombe's develop- ment in depth. But this study provides an introduction to the major features of its growth up to the First World War, from a tiny watering- place in the late eighteenth century, expanding more rapidly with improved communications in the 1810s and 1820s and particularly the 1870s and 1880s towards its height at the turn of the century.[1]

The origins of the North Devon holiday industry, in common with other south and south-west coast resorts, lies in the increasing demand of the eighteenth-century leisured classes for whom the spas at Bath, Tunbridge, Cheltenham and Clifton in the south and west, and Harrogate, Matlock and Buxton in the north, were no longer exclusive preserves. By the second half of the century prosperous commercial centres such as Bristol and Exeter, and many smaller provincial towns, produced a sufficient flow of visitors in search of health and relaxation to enable numbers of tiny fishing ports and ship-building centres dotted along the coasts of the south-west to transform themselves into fashionable watering-places.

1   This article is based on part of my unpublished University of Wales MA dissertation on 'The development of Ilfracombe as a resort in the nineteenth century' (1978).

This change of function became for most a necessity, since by the early nineteenth century the herring fishery, a mainstay of the Bristol Channel coast economy, was in decline, and, with the growth of manufacturing centres in the north and midlands, the industrial and commercial importance of the south-west began to wane. The West Riding rather than the West Country became the principal producer of woollens, and Liverpool succeeded Bristol as the leading west coast port.

Although about 70 miles from Bristol by sea, Ilfracombe felt the effects of this decline more than most. But its development as a watering-place prevented the total decay that followed wherever economic diversification was impossible. Indeed the rise of the holiday towns, in contrast to the depopulation of the rural areas, is one of the main themes in the social and economic history of nineteenth century Devon. For most of the eighteenth century Ilfracombe had remained largely as Defoe described it in the 1720s, 'a town of good trade populous and rich, all of which is owing to its having a very good harbour and road for ships, and where ships from Ireland often put in, when in bad weather, they cannot, without the extremest hazard, run into the mouth of the Taw'.[1] In addition to the herring fishery a substantial part of the population was engaged in other traditional maritime occupations, notably piloting, shipbuilding and repair. Its sheltered position at the southern mouth of the Bristol Channel gave the port a key role in the sailing era as a harbour of refuge, and vessels driven in by Atlantic gales provided a lucrative source of employment, frequently supplemented by the smuggling and wrecking activities for which the coast was notorious. By the 1750s, according to Dean Milles of Exeter, 'coals from Wales and mackerel and herring' were among the most important trades, but agricultural produce was also shipped to Bristol and the rapidly expanding South Wales industrial areas.[2]

Although sea-bathing had become fashionable on the South Devon coast, no mention is made of resort activities at this time in the north of the county. Exmouth and Teignmouth had already developed reputations as exclusive resorts, while by the 1790s Sidmouth could boast royal patronage.[3] By the late eighteenth century, however, Ilfracombe was also

1   Daniel Defoe, *A tour through the whole island of Great Britain* (1724-6, Penguin, 1971 ed.) p.248.

2   Milles Devonshire MSS; Parochial Collections and Returns, 1753, Bodleian Library, Oxford (microfilm copy in West Country Studies Library, Exeter).

3   On the early development of the South Devon resorts see William G Hoskins, *A new survey of England : Devon* (Collins, 1954) pp.117-20, 386-7, 449-50, 477-8, 491-2, 500-3; John A Bulley, 'Teignmouth as a seaside resort (before the coming of the railway)', *Transactions of the Devonshire Association*, 88 (1956) pp.145-6; E A G Clark, *The estuarine ports of the Exe and Teign,* unpublished University of London PhD thesis, 1956; Eric R Delderfield, *Exmouth milestones* (Exmouth : Raleigh Press, 1948) p.36; Gordon D and Edith G C Griffiths, *History of Teignmouth* (Teignmouth : Brunswick Press, 1965) pp.34-5.

emerging as a watering-place. In 1788 the *Exeter Flying Post* reported
the town 'remarkably full of genteel company being resorted to by
members of very respectable families from most parts of the country.
What pleases strangers most is the conveniency of the bathing machines,
and the great attention of the townspeople to accommodate them'.[1] From
the 1790s Ilfracombe was frequently described as 'a pleasant and
convenient place for bathing and much resorted to by the gentry for
that purpose'.[2]

But it was scenery as well as the sea-bathing, recommended increasingly by eighteenth-century doctors for its curative properties,
which attracted the early tourists. Until the last decades of the
century travellers to Devon had paid little attention to the remote
north coast, but with the rediscovery of the natural beauties of England
and Wales came a new interest quite absent from the earlier travel writings of Defoe or Bishop Pococke. From the 1760s and 1770s the mountains
of the Lake District and Snowdonia had become popular excursion centres
for fashionable society. Soon the scenic splendours of Devonshire and
its craggy northern coastline also captured the romantic imagination.
By the 1790s Ilfracombe was being described in early guide books as
'truly romantic', the author of one, W G Maton, marvelling at 'the
magnificent sweep of the Bristol Channel with the Welsh coast beyond'.[3]
The closure of the Continent during the French Wars gave this movement
further impetus, and by the early nineteenth century the cliff coast
between Ilfracombe and the twin villages of Lynton and Lynmouth was
becoming known as 'the English Switzerland', attracting the acclaim of
Coleridge, Wordsworth, Southey, Shelley and other Romantics. Such
publicity was to prove invaluable.

Despite some increase in Ilfracombe's maritime importance during
the War its population experienced great hardships, manifested in food
riots such as in 1801 against the shipment of barley to Bristol. Recent
research has uncovered widespread distress in Devon during these years,
and in Ilfracombe the situation grew more desperate with the return of
peace.[4] The herring fishery had become notoriously unreliable; Bristol

---

1   *Exeter Flying Post*, 17 July 1788.

2   *Universal British Directory*, III (1791) 417.

3   W G Maton, *Observations on the western counties*, (1794-6) in Richard
     Pearse-Chope ed. *Early tours in Devon and Cornwall* (Newton Abbot :
     David & Charles, 1967) p.277. On the movement in general see Esther
     Moir, *The discovery of England : the English tourist 1540 to 1840*
     (Routledge & Kegan Paul, 1964) esp. chap.2.

4   Grahame Farr, *Ships and harbours of Exmoor* (Dulverton : Exmoor Press,
     1970) p.14; Roger Wells, 'The revolt of the South West, 1800-1801 :
     a study in English popular protest', *Social History*, 6 (1977) 713-44;
     J Bohstedt, 'Riots in England 1790-1810, with special reference to
     Devon', unpublished Harvard University D Phil thesis, 1972.

was declining in importance and as steam power revolutionised coastal
trade the Channel ports also stagnated. Ilfracombe's ship registrations
fell dramatically, and numbers of crews migrated to the South Wales
ports to join the Welsh mineral boom or sought employment elsewhere.
Boat-building and ship repair consequently fell off. Ironically in its
virtual destruction of the coastal sailing trade, steam power acted as
a catalyst on the development of the watering-place. The only branch
of trade to increase was the number of visitors brought to the town by
the new steam packets from the early 1820s.[1]

By 1828 T H Cornish in his *Sketch of the rise and progress of the
principal towns of the North of Devon,* commented:

> The families of distinction that have been in and about Ilfracombe
> for some months past seem loath to quit at present though
> September is well nigh spent. We confess we do not feel surprised
> ....steamers and pleasure yachts crowd the coast in every direction
> during the summer months in quick succession. The constant and
> rapid communication with Ireland, Wales and Bristol has brought a
> most surprising change....and since the different steam packets
> have been plying to and fro from Bristol and Swansea and so on, the
> busy arrivals and departures have been witnessed with no small
> gratification by the authorities.[2]

It is impossible in the absence of traffic figures to measure the
impact of these improvements on the town's development. But as the
periodic reports of excursion arrivals at summer weekends in the local
press show, the steam packets were crucial to the resort's growth.
Ilfracombe was separated not only from Bristol and South Wales by sea,
but from faster growing towns like Exeter, Plymouth and Devonport in
the south of the county. In 1827 the overland journey from Barnstaple
to Bristol still took nineteen hours, those to South Devon relatively
even longer, and pack animals remained the most efficient means of
transporting merchandise overland.[3] Its geographical isolation accounted for the slow development of the holiday industry and water transport
was to remain vital even after the arrival of the railway.

Ilfracombe itself was little more than a village in the early nineteenth century; in 1811 its population was still under two thousand,
though the number of houses had increased by over eighty in the previous
sixty years. In the course of the next century the population rose more
rapidly, especially, as shown in the following table, in the 1810s and
1820s and again, after a temporary lull, from the late 1860s and 1870s -
a growth rate reflected in the town's physical expansion.[4]

---

1   Farr, *Ships and harbours,* pp.20, 22, and his *West country passenger
     steamers* (Prescot : Stephenson, 2nd ed. 1967) pp.71-3, 78, 90-3.

2   Thomas H Cornish, *Sketch of the rise and progress of the principal
     towns of the north of Devon* (Bristol, 1828) pp.28-9.

3   *North Devon Journal,* 25 May 1827.

4   Milles MSS; Census of England and Wales.

Table 1

POPULATION AND HOUSING, ILFRACOMBE PARISH 1801-1911

	Population	% Change	Houses	% Change
1801	1838			
1811	1934	5.2	444	
1821	2622	35.6	531	19.6
1831	3201	22.1	681	28.2
1841	3679	14.9	795	16.7
1851	3677	- 0.1	852	7.2
1861	3851	4.7	857	0.6
1871	4721	22.6	1042	21.6
1881	6255	32.5	1242	19.2
1891	7692	23.0	1738	39.9
1901	8557	11.2	2142	23.2
1911	8935	4.4		

Source: Census Reports

Like many West Country resorts that developed from fishing villages the early nineteenth century settlement straggled along a single street from the harbour uphill to the parish church that marked the traditional boundary of development, and the focal point for routes to the local markets of Barnstaple and Bideford. The small harbour dominated Ilfracombe's urban geography and its economy, and the pattern of land-ownership, upon which the growth of the resort depended, was governed by its traditional maritime and agricultural activities. But already land was being given over to the building of holiday accommodation, initially in the form of elegant terraces and villas for wealthy season visitors.

Later on it was hoped that many would return as residents and to-wards the end of the nineteenth century Ilfracombe gained a reputation as a retirement centre catering especially for gentry and military and other professional families. Though, with its romantic scenery and promenades, the town also became popular with honeymooners. Indeed the pattern of growth from the 1820s reflected the early development of the resort in the heady atmosphere of romanticism and Francophobia of the war years, when the Continent was closed to English visitors. Ilfracombe grew up as much as a centre from which to explore the surrounding country-side as a health resort; though the recognition that sea-air could be as important an aid to recuperation as immersion enabled it to exploit its north-facing position and 'bracing' climate - hitherto neglected by medical fashion - in the treatment of various pulmonary disorders. Accommodation was provided higher and higher up the slopes above the town where the freshness of the air, and splendour of the views, increased with the price of lodgings.

There was no room in Ilfracombe, however, for planning on the grand scale as at Torquay. The town itself occupied only a small part of the 5583 acre parish, and most of the estates upon which development might take place were parts of much larger purely agricultural tracts. Often the gradients involved made building impractical. In the course of the nineteenth century Ilfracombe nonetheless achieved great celebrity while physically remaining very compact. By comparison with Torquay it had little impact on the local landscape, though this was not often appreciated by contemporaries, and from the 1860s fears were constantly raised that bricks and mortar were engulfing the surrounding country-side and destroying the very scenery that had led to expansion in the first place. It is this restricted pattern of development before 1914 that gives the town its peculiarly Victorian character, and part of its value as a case study in resort growth.

The tithe map of 1840 clearly reveals the fragmentation of land-ownership early on.[1] Within the area built up by 1914 only one estate (the Torrs) exceeded 100 acres, 15 others were over 15 acres and 25 between 1 and 5. The vast majority - 54 - were under one acre, and most were scattered in several parts of the town, affording little opportunity for more than piecemeal development. The larger holdings were almost all in the hands of local gentlemen or yeomen farmers. Within the town itself the lord of the manor, Sir Bourchier Palk Wrey, owned over 100 properties, including the harbour, pier, boatyard, Lantern, Compass and Capstone Hills, as well as much of the land above the town.[2] The Wreys were summer residents only at this time, however. Several interrelated families, such as the Lees and Vyes, magistrates and bankers, and other wealthy individuals retired from distinguished military careers, like Admirals Bowen and Down, or civil servants like Sir James Meek exerted considerable influence in the community not only through their property, but in the social and political leadership they provided in the absence of a more formal system of local government.

Sir Bourchier himself undoubtedly took a paternal interest in the town, rebuilding the harbour pier after its destruction by storms in the 1820s (his father had done the same in 1760), and enlarging it again before he died. As Chairman of the Barnstaple Turnpike Trust in 1828-9, he helped steer to completion the new coach road between Exeter, Barnstaple and Ilfracombe, and backed numerous other improvements. But unlike his close relatives the Palks, who did so much to develop Torquay, he played a very limited role in Ilfracombe's growth as a resort. Others were much more active in the development of the watering-place, promoting new buildings and amenities. The main impetus in the early years came

1   Ilfracombe Tithe Survey Map and Apportionment, 1840. (Copy in Ilfracombe Museum). The survey area was based on the approximate extent of development before 1914.

2   Sir Bourchier Palk Wrey, 1788-1879; 8th baronet, J.P. etc. The estate was subsequently administered in trust because of the insanity of his successor. On the role of the Palks see Percy Russell, *A history of Torquay* (Torquay : Natural History Society, 1960) pp.86-90. See also, W H Rogers, 'The Barnstaple turnpike trust', *Transactions of the Devonshire Association*, 74 (1942) 144-51, 162.

from small local speculators. Sometimes the landowner developed the property himself as at Down Place, but what usually seems to have occurred, as at other watering-places like Dawlish, was the sale of individual plots with restrictions as to use and appearance by covenants and ground-rent charges by the original owners.[1]

As the number of new addresses listed as lodgings in the directories show, most of the early resort building was for letting to wealthy residents and visitors. During the first quarter of the nineteenth century accommodation was to be found mostly on or near the quay. The first hotels, the Britannia and Packet, were as much for ships' passengers as holiday visitors, and it is also indicative of the way Ilfracombe developed from a fishing port that lodging-house keepers were frequently the wives or widows of fishermen and mariners for whom few other livelihoods were available. Facilities were often primitive: Fanny Burney, visiting the town as an old woman in 1817, removed from the quayside apartments kept by a captain's widow because of the stench of the harbour at low tide. But visitors were increasingly accommodated in other parts of the town. The radical M.P., Sir Francis Burdett, for example, took one of builder Thomas Chiswell's houses in the High Street, on the north side of which many lodgings were being put up to take advantage of the fine sea views.[2]

The census figures show the first significant increase in building to have taken place in the 1810s and 1820s. It was in these years that Ilfracombe's terraces were constructed. Their architectural style and the names Coburg, Regent and Waterloo Terraces and Caroline Place are all redolent of the Regency and subsequent period. Between 1811 and 1821 87 houses were completed, and another 150 by 1831. By the end of the decade the unprecedented popularity of the resort, reflecting the improved communications, was stimulating considerable speculative activity. As T H Cornish noted, 'new buildings are in such a state of forwardness which will....prove not only profitable to the owners but commensurate with the rise and opulence of the town'.[3] The town was indeed becoming more opulent. By the 1830s a start had been made on Ilfracombe's four most elegant 'Georgian' terraces. The finest, Adelaide Terrace, named after the Queen who, as Duchess of Clarence,had visited the town in 1827, was built at one time by Thomas Chiswell. The other three were constructed in stages over a number of years, and by different builders, which accounts for their variety of style. Montpellier Terrace, begun in the mid-1820s, was soon followed by Hillsborough and Coronation Terraces, the last incorporating much needed

1   Ewart Johns, 'Urban design in Dawlish and Chelston', in Kenneth J Gregory and William L D Ravenhill, eds. *Exeter essays in geography* (Exeter UP, 1971) pp.201-3.

2   *Ilfracombe Observer*, 26 April 1890; *Ilfracombe Chronicle*, 12 November 1904.

3   cf. Table 1, and Cornish, *Principal towns*, pp.24-30.

Public Assembly, Ball and Billiard Rooms.[1]

The market in development land remained vigorous throughout the 1830s and local speculative activity also extended to the provision of amenities. Pressure on bathing facilities led to the tunnelling of the cliff and opening out of separate bathing beaches for ladies and gentlemen at Crewkhorne in 1836 by the recently formed Sea-Bathing Company.[2] Segregated bathing helped set the high moral tone which long remained a cardinal feature of holiday-making in Ilfracombe. The Doric bath-house at the tunnel entrance became one of the town's social centres near which in Bath Place and along Northfield to the High Street, villas were built in a variety of styles, among them the neo-classical stuccoed Northfield House and the Gothic Runnymede villa where Charles Kingsley later stayed. By the 1840s it seemed to contemporaries that the town had been transformed. Overall between 1821 and 1851, despite the setbacks of the late 1840s, the housing stock increased by over 60 per cent. It is impossible to measure the capital investment in building during this period, but the press estimated it to be in the region of £150,000, almost all of it from local sources.[3]

Ilfracombe also experienced 'the spirit of town improvement' of the 1830s. As at Torquay and other resorts much of this was purely private in inception. Traditionally Ilfracombe's local government had been left to the Vestry overseers and waywardens, and officers, like the Port Reeve, elected at the Annual Courts Leet and Baron, the last vestiges of manorial authority. But with the growth of the town's reputation as a health and holiday resort new local government authorities became essential if the overcrowding and insanitary conditions of inland towns were to be avoided. Early in the century few authorities considered it their responsibility to aid the development of the resorts directly, and the provision of amenities was generally left to private enterprise. The town was lit by gas in 1837, for example, three years after Barnstaple and Torquay, but earlier than Teignmouth and Dawlish. Like the Sea-Bathing Company, the Ilfracombe Gas Company was the inspiration of local entrepreneurs, businessmen like the publisher John Banfield, and professional gentlemen like the surgeons Thomas Stabb and John Jones, its chairman.[4]

1   Various deeds kindly loaned by the owners; John Banfield, *A guide to Ilfracombe...* (1st ed. Ilfracombe, 1830) p.5.

2   *North Devon Journal*, 15 September 1836; Banfield, *Guide to Ilfracombe*, 1836 ed. p.12.

3   *North Devon Journal*, 25 May 1848; cf. Table 1.

4   John Banfield, printer and bookseller, son-in-law of Richard Trevithick, came to Ilfracombe c.1820, d.1870; he supported many voluntary and commercial activities including the Cottage Garden Society, Odd-Fellows Lodge and Freehold Land and Investment Society; he was a member of the Local Board of Health 1851-2. Thomas

But private initiative alone was shown to be inadequate in the key areas of highway administration and public health. Communications to and through the town were appalling; wheeled traffic was still relatively uncommon, and donkeys and sedan chairs remained the main means of street transport. Responsibility for the badly-needed widening and resurfacing of the streets, however, was ill-defined. The Barnstaple Turnpike Trust, long the major body responsible for roads in North Devon, had obtained special powers to improve and maintain Ilfracombe's roads to meet the needs of visitors by an Act of 1827, though the parish also retained its street cleaning and related functions.[1] Supervision of the proposed works was vested in a body of local trustees, but the work of this *ad hoc* Town Improvement Committee inevitably stretched beyond road repair, and for a number of years it became in effect the town's chief local government authority.

By the 1840s, however, its narrow interpretation of its role led to friction with the townspeople and visitors, especially since the failure of the Trust to recoup its earlier expenditure in the town prevented essential sanitary improvements. Visitors' complaints of 'small pools of stagnant water, the heaps of rubbish and decayed vegetable matter in every stage of decomposition' had been common in the local press since the early 1830s, yet the town had escaped the cholera epidemic of 1831-2.[2] In the 1840s it was to be less fortunate. Despite an attempt to reconstitute the Committee in 1842 and provide voluntary contributions for cleaning the streets and improving the public walks, it became clear that vital improvements in public health, to enable Ilfracombe to maintain its reputation, would have to come directly from the townspeople themselves. Their long campaign for an Improvement Act like that of Torquay was, however, swept up in the clamour for effective health authorities to deal with the national cholera epidemic of 1848-9.[3]

Stabb, MD, d.1878, came to Ilfracombe from Torquay in 1823. He became a director of the Ilfracombe Sea-Bathing, Gas and Hotel Companies, and the first chairman of the Local Board of Health from 1851-9. John Jones, MD, d.1866. Fortescue Lodge; also epitomised much local entrepreneurial activity. He was chairman of the Ilfracombe Sea-Bathing Company and the Gas Company, and backed numerous other improvements. He became a member of the Local Board from 1851, and its chairman 1859-65.

1   The Barnstaple Turnpike Trust was established in 1763, with borrowing powers for 21 years. These were renewed and extended in 1827, 7 and 8 Geo IV, to include responsibility for Ilfracombe's streets. *North Devon Journal*, 23 March 1827; Rogers, 'Barnstaple turnpike trust', pp.144, 146-7, 149-51.

2   *North Devon Journal*, 1 September 1831.

3   Public Record Office (PRO) MH13/99, correspondence of General Board of Health (with Ilfracombe authorities), 12 April 1848 – 15 October 1849, and subsequently with Ilfracombe Local Board of Health; *North Devon Journal*, 22 February 1849, 21 June 1849, et seq.

The local situation was exacerbated by the national economic depression in the 1840s. With heavy unemployment in traditional occupations the trickle of emigrants from North Devon became a flood. Between 500 and 600 left the area in the first two months of 1841 alone.[1] Like resorts in other parts of the country in the 1840s Ilfracombe's parish population ceased to grow. The slow decay of the employment structure brought about by the decline of the herring fishery and coastal sail took on a new significance. In the hard winter of 1842-3 relief works were provided by subscription to overcome the hardships of an unbalanced seasonal economy. The Capstone Promenade was the first of these and epitomises the dilemma facing the town. Relief works could only be a temporary solution. The holiday industry provided the only alternative. Ilfracombe's future lay in the provision of amenities for as many visitors of the right sort as possible.

Several good seasons delayed action, but by the end of the 1840s the twin problems of public health and unemployment reached crisis proportions. In February 1849 prominent townsmen, spurred on by Charles Kingsley, who had come to Ilfracombe to recover from one of his periodic breakdowns, urged the town to provide a 'labour fund' and tighten its 'sanitary slackness'. Cholera intensified their efforts. But local government in its existing form remained powerless to act and mounting public pressure culminated in the application of the Public Health Act of 1848 and the establishment of a Local Board of Health, under which Ilfracombe at last acquired a municipal authority strong enough to give the town a lead in the change of direction so long overdue.[2]

The Local Board of Health dominated the development of the town in the second half of the century. For over forty years until the takeover by the Urban District Council in 1894 it exercised control over the sanitary and other municipal affairs of the locality. Like most Victorian local authorities the Board was periodically subjected to attacks from 'Economy' parties of ratepayers, and progress was often slow and hindered by opposition to what was regarded as extravagant expenditure in the narrow interests of the holiday industry. Nevertheless it proved crucial in stimulating and controlling the growth of the resort. Its first priority - the improvement of the town's drainage and water supply - was achieved by the building of new sewage works in 1853, and, after many delays, a reservoir in 1866.[3] The continuing improvement of water and

1   *North Devon Journal*, 11 March 1841. Advertisements for and reports of emigrants leaving the area appeared frequently from this time to the early 1850s.

2   Thomas W Rammell, *Report to the General Board of Health on...the sanitary condition...of Ilfracombe* (1850); *North Devon Journal*, 29 November 1849; 19 September 1850 et seq.

3   Minutes, Ilfracombe Local Board of Health, Devon Record Office (DRO) R2458 A/C 1, 19 October 1852, 4 November 1852, 14 June 1853; PRO MH13/99, 24 December 1852, 29 April 1853, 14 July 1860, 15 August 1866.

drainage facilities was accompanied by an equally energetic pursuit of
its other responsibilities, and through an increasingly stringent code
of bye-laws the Board came to regulate nearly every aspect of the
town's life, laying the guide-lines for the future expansion of the
holiday industry.

The town's economic recovery from the stagnation of the late
1840s and early 1850s was, however, an arduous process. Though local
subscriptions in 1850-1 enabled several families to emigrate on assisted
passages, with the average agricultural labourer's wage at 7s per week
emigration was out of the question for the majority, and the new local
authority resorted once more to relief works. Sandy Lane, the present
Highfield Road, was completed as a scenic drive by unemployed labourers
in 1854, providing a future growth point. But for the nation as a
whole the 1850s introduced a period of unprecedented prosperity, and as
the effects of the mid-Victorian boom gradually spread to North Devon
confidence was restored, stimulating a new period of growth. For
Ilfracombe, as for other holiday resorts, one of the key features of
this was the expansion of the railway network.

Its role in increasing the flow of visitors had already been demonstrated in the 1840s. Brunel's broad-gauge Great Western Railway had
reached Bristol in 1841 and in 1844 was extended to Exeter by the Bristol
and Exeter Railway Company. The upsurge of visitors to previously in-
accessible watering-places was felt immediately. As the tracks penetrated
further into the South-West traditional coach routes were abandoned and
services adjusted to new time-tables operated from the nearest railhead.
Initially, with the opening of the line to Bridgwater and Taunton,
Ilfracombe benefitted greatly, receiving numbers of visitors previously
unwilling to travel to the resort by stage or steam packet alone.[1] But
when the line reached Exeter in 1844 most travellers continued on to
the south coast, and within two years the South Devon Railway Company
extended the main line to Dawlish and Teignmouth, and a branch on to
Torquay by 1848. Ilfracombe did its best to compete, but, despite the
ititial operating set-backs, the new line gave the south coast resorts a
commanding lead.[2]

North Devon had already made an attempt to gain railway communication
with the rest of the network. As early as 1836 a North and South Devon
Railway was projected, followed in 1837 by the revival of an Exeter-
Crediton scheme providing for an extension to Barnstaple. The first proposal to include Ilfracombe was mooted in 1844. Yet despite several
grandiose schemes during the Railway Mania of 1845-7, North Devon remained without a branch until 1854, when, after one of the most bitter and
protracted battles in the war between the broad-gauge Great Western,

1   *North Devon Journal*, 30 July 1841; David St John Thomas, *A regional
     history of the railways of Great Britain*, Vol.1, *The West Country*,
     (Phoenix, 1960) p.11.

2   Thomas, *Railways of Britain*, pp.42-50, 62.

Bristol and Exeter, and South Devon Railway Companies and the narrow-
gauge South Western Railway, a line was opened as far as Barnstaple by
the contractor Thomas Brassey. The impact on Ilfracombe was immediate
and considerable. Coach services to the resort from Barnstaple were
intensified, and the town was inundated with visitors. A shortage of
accommodation soon became apparent and encouraged some renewal of
building activity. But more important in the long run was the opening
of a branch to Ilfracombe itself. This prerequisite for large-scale
expansion, however, was to be delayed twenty years.

Though Bideford was reached from Barnstaple in 1855, two
Ilfracombe schemes in 1854 were presented too late for that parliamentary session and subsequent plans all foundered on financial and
managerial difficulties. Not until 1860, with the completion of the
South Western Railway's alternative route to Exeter from Waterloo and
its acquisition of running powers to Barnstaple did Ilfracombe's
prospects improve. But from this point the history of the newly-formed
Ilfracombe Railway Company replicated on a more protracted but equally
ferocious scale the conflicts of the Railway Mania. Indeed the inter-
minable wrangling of the broad- and narrow-gauge companies in North
Devon provides a classic example of the monumental territorial self-
interest of the large Victorian railway companies at the expense of
the area they quarrelled over, and the feebleness of the government
to control them.[1] Controversy centred on the question of which of two
routes should be adopted, the western coastal line via Braunton that
was eventually chosen, or a shorter but hillier eastern one via
Bittadon that would run closer to the harbour. Opinion in the town
remained bitterly divided over both this and the company to back. In
1863 the defeat of the Ilfracombe Railway Bill proposing the western
route provoked street riots. All the more ironic because the South
Western, recognising the growing importance of Ilfracombe, began
advertising its West of England summer express service for 'Exeter and
Ilfracombe', though the last part of the journey was by coach. Further
valuable time was lost by the failure of the chief promoter, the Exeter
solicitor, Robert Wreford, following the collapse of his South Devon
speculations. Altogether eight bills were introduced and six acts
passed by the contestants before construction finally began in 1871.
Even then labour shortages and engineering difficulties increased costs
and delayed completion, and the broad-gauge companies continued to contemplate a second branch to the town. Not until 1885 was the route
issue finally settled when a junction at Barnstaple from the Devon and
Somerset line to the South Western railway and a mixed-gauge line to

1   Jack Simmons, 'South Western v. Great Western : railway competition
     in Devon and Cornwall', *Journal of Transport History,* 4 (1959) 18-
     19; Ronald A Williams, *The London and South Western railway* (Newton
     Abbot : David & Charles, 1963) Vol.1, pp.107-18; Edward T MacDermot
     (ed. Charles R Clinker), *History of the Great Western railway*
     (Ian Allan, 1964 ed.) Vol.II, pp.77-81, 84-5.

Ilfracombe was authorised.[1]

The coming of the railway produced a mass influx of visitors, but in anticipation of its completion Ilfracombe had already begun to prosper once again from the late 1850s. Building accelerated and the demand for new villa accommodation from the wealthy mid-Victorian upper and middle classes began a change in the town's physical appearance. On the slopes above the town the Hostle Park estate was begun in 1856, one villa being taken for the 1858 season by members of the Rothschild family. But by far the most important residential development of these years was the floating by local businessmen, professionals and gentlemen of the Ilfracombe Joint Stock Land and Investment Company in 1860. The Torrs Park Company, as it was known locally, aimed to turn Ilfracombe into 'the Brighton of the South West' by building luxury villa accommodation on the 'Torrs' to the west of the town. In this it was typical of many land companies in the development of select residential estates at fashionable watering-places, extending the earlier work of individual landowners in creating and maintaining high-status areas well away from the encroachments of more plebeian visitors.[2] It set the tone for the town's future development and started the move away from its traditional east-west axis parallel to the High Street. A new line was now emerging, running from the north-east to the south-west and extending towards the future railway terminus; this necessitated a new route to the harbour and sea which eventually became the town's new thoroughfare, Wilder Road. Architecturally, as Pevsner has shown, the transition from the elegant Georgian and Early-Victorian terraced dwellings that had so far characterised the resort was also marked by the completion in 1857 of the church of St Philip and St James near the front to cater for the increased number of respectable visitors.[3] Henceforward Ilfracombe acquired the High-Victorian Gothic flavour that it still retains.

But the new luxury villas catered for only a small proportion of the visitors. The social range of holiday-makers who could afford to reach even the more isolated resorts was beginning to widen and rows of terraced lodging houses were also provided, offering rooms from 5s to £10 per week.[4] The most serious deficiency in Ilfracombe's holiday accommodation compared to centres like Torquay, however, was in the provision of luxury hotels. The three existing establishments hardly merited that title, though two claimed royal patronage: the Royal Britannia, favoured

1   Frank E Box, 'The Barnstaple and Ilfracombe railway', *Railway Magazine*, 45 (1919) 408-14; (1920) 24-9; Williams, *London and South Western*, Vol.II (1973) pp.229-36.

2   *North Devon Journal*, 15 July 1858. On the role of land companies see, J A Barrett, *The seaside towns of England and Wales*, unpublished University of London PhD thesis (1958).

3   Nikolaus Pevsner, *The buildings of England* (Penguin, 1952) p.107.

4   *North Devon Journal*, 27 July 1849, 24 July 1856; *Bright's Intelligencer*, 2 May 1861.

by an out-of-season stay by the Prince of Wales in 1856, and the Royal Clarence visited by Queen Adelaide in 1827. With the Pier Hotel the Royal Britannia shared a thriving trade in overnight accommodation for those disembarking from boats, while the Royal Clarence became the town's major staging point.

But when an ambitious Ilfracombe Hotel and Esplanade Company was floated in 1863 by a consortium of those backing the railway it was met with derision. Its giant hotel scheme was, however, a brilliant gamble to capitalise on the expected railway and put the town among the first rank of watering-places. It took some time to convince investors of the scheme's merits, and the 200-bedroom Italianate structure on the resort's prime site was only completed in 1867. For the first time most of the capital came from outside the locality. By the time the railway opened in 1874, 39 per cent of the shares were from London, 18 per cent from Ilfracombe and 40 per cent from the rest of Devon. The hotel, opened in advance of the railway, set the pattern for the development of the town in the last quarter of the nineteenth century, years of unprecedented popularity and prosperity.[1] From the first it attracted many famous visitors, including the future Kaiser Wilhelm in 1878, and from its inception it was regarded as a barometer of the resort's fortunes. Its gross receipts, as presented in Table 2, provide a crude index of the seasonal fluctuations facing a seaside-town that depended upon good weather and national prosperity. From the late 1880s, after a period of considerable growth, it also met increasing competition from 'private hotels', catering for middle class families on the more economical 'boarding-house' principle. It turned to wealthy foreign visitors, especially Americans like the Vanderbilts who stayed in 1884, but also developed inclusive 'package' holidays at special rates, and sought to attract conferences out of season, eventually helping to seal its own fate by installing a garage in 1906.[2]

From 1870 with the completion of much new building, the establishment of the Hotel and the anticipated arrival of the railway, holiday-making in Ilfracombe entered its modern phase, and as the numbers of visitors increased the resort took on a new physical and social configuration. In 1869 it was estimated that over 40,000 summer visitors were staying at the resort, and by the 1890s the local press reported 30,000 visitors to the town at peak times. The 'Fashionable Arrival Lists' printed each week revealed the same upward trends.[3] By the late 1880s the pattern of holiday-making was also beginning to change. Higher real wages increased competition between the new pleasure steamer companies, often running in conjunction with the major railways from Bristol or the South Wales ports, and improved rail facilities brought a mass clientele from the Midlands and North of England. Most visitors were still middle class, although in the 1880s and 1890s cheaper excursion fares, through running on the rail-

1   PRO BT 31/30721, Shareholders' Lists, Ilfracombe Hotel Company.

2   *Ilfracombe Gazette*, 9 August 1884; *North Devon Journal*, 3 November 1891; *Ilfracombe Chronicle*, 29 December 1906.

3   *Ilfracombe Observer*, 6 December 1892.

Table 2

ILFRACOMBE HOTEL COMPANY, GROSS RECEIPTS 1867-1914

	£		£		£		£
1867	8192	1879	14480	1891	17104	1903	13652
1868	13480	1880	17879	1892	16745	1904	11186
1869	14016	1881	18868	1893	17581	1905	11736
1870	14906	1882	19686	1894	14457	1906	12549
1871	16005	1883	18386	1895	16567	1907	11924
1872	14864	1884	20009	1896	13607	1908	11459
1873	13380	1885	18407	1897	14172	1909	12479
1874	15351	1886	18190	1898	13386	1910	12899
1875	16060	1887	18359	1899	14974	1911	12154
1876	18273	1888	15786	1900	13856	1912	12029
1877	15326	1889	17232	1901	12715	1913	13573
1878	15928	1890	19572	1902	14014		

Source: Receipts from Annual Reports and Accounts in local
press.

ways, and especially the ending of the broad gauge, brought much of Devon
within the reach of more affluent workers who now began to demand a
different sort of holiday from that provided in the more popular
Lancashire and North Wales resorts. Ilfracombe had largely been insulated
from the more 'undesirable' elements. Day trips from Bristol were not
usual until the 1890s; but the South Wales industrial towns were a mere
three hours away by steamer, and, since the first half of the century,
thousands of iron, steel and tinplate workers had been brought over on
Sundays and holidays during the season, crowding out the town and often
returning the worse for drink. Indeed after the Welsh Sunday Closing Act
of 1881 so many came over on drinking trips that these floating beershops
were banned.[1]

Though the town's response to the 'Merry Cymri' who brought much-
needed revenue but threatened to lower the tone of the resort remained
ambivalent, Ilfracombe's leading business interests had, nevertheless,
begun to sense the need to provide greater amenities to attract a wider
but still respectable clientele to the resort. Initially it had depended
almost entirely on its natural attractions, scenic grandeur and healthy
climate. In an age when the function of watering-places was primarily

1   eg *Ilfracombe Chronicle*, 10 July 1894. (Estimate of 10,000 visitors
     weekly from the Midlands by steamer); *North Devon Journal*, 2 July
     1896; Select Committee, House of Commons, Ilfracombe Harbour and
     Improvement Bill, 1905, Mins. of Evidence (J C Clarke), p.22, DRO RG
     2458/H18. See also W R Lambert, 'The Welsh Sunday closing act 1881',
     Welsh History Review, 6 (1972-3) 161-89.

recuperative, adequate sea-bathing facilities and the usual genteel diversions found at the spas were all that was required. These were provided at Ilfracombe in the first half of the century; hot and cold baths at the 'Tunnels' after 1836; Assembly Rooms including facilities for dancing and billiards at Coronation Terrace by the early 1830s, regattas and flower shows and a series of soirées and balls which annually made up the major events of the social calendar. But apart from the Capstone Promenade and other walks few amenities were added before the late 1860s.

From mid-century, however, the Devon resorts had grown greatly in favour with the Victorian middle classes, partly as a result of the new mania for natural history inspired by writers like Philip Gosse and G H Lewes. The latter's *Sea-side Studies,* published after a holiday in Ilfracombe and Tenby with George Eliot in 1856, opened up a whole new seashore world for collectors and classifiers of shells, rockpools and inter-tidal biology. The narrow lanes of the North Devon countryside also enjoyed immense popularity with visitors intent on collecting and pressing local wild flowers, and especially ferns. Indeed Ilfracombe became the centre of a minor cult of fern hunters following the publication by Charlotte Chanter, the daughter of the Vicar of Ilfracombe, of *Ferny Combes* in 1856. But above all the North Devon coast was becoming famous for its literary associations, especially the works of her uncle, Charles Kingsley, in particular *Westward Ho!* first published in 1855.

The arrival of the railway and enlargement of the pier in the early 1870s to cater for increasing numbers of sea-borne visitors, however, ushered in a new range of amusements and entertainments that in the twentieth century have become the hall-marks of the British sea-side holiday industry - not that Ilfracombe ceased to be other than a respectable and sometimes overbearingly stuffy holiday centre before 1914. Any hint of impropriety was quickly stifled by the combined disapproval of churches and chapels and the strict code of local bye-laws which forbade such immoralities as Sunday concerts, cheap-jacks parading their wares on the beach, and mixed-bathing, banned until the early 1900s.

But as the number of visitors continued to grow, more popular entertainments slowly appeared. Already in the 1860s the first steps had been taken to advertise the town, and extend the season.[1] By the 1870s several promotional schemes were being put forward, including those for an 'entertainments' complex' on Ropery Meadow, beside the Ilfracombe Hotel, that at one point included an aquarium and roller-skating rink. The Hotel itself led the way with a covered sea-water bathing pool in 1880, advertised at its opening as the largest in the South-West, and aquatic carnivals and swimming galas became a major attraction in the town. By the end of the 1880s concerts were being given at the Oxford Hall, off the High Street, and several of the newer hotels, together with

---

1   The Town Advertising Committee was established in 1862. *North Devon Journal,* 25 June 1862, 24 July 1862.

both official and unofficial open-air performances by touring bands in
the season. But the most important addition in these years was the
Victoria Pavilion, the winter garden under Capstone Hill, built to
commemorate the Golden Jubilee. Even this soon proved to be too small
for the summer crowds who demanded concerts almost nightly in high
summer. At the beginning of the new century shows and concerts were
being given at various hotels, the Kursaal on the pier, and the
Alexandra Theatre opened by the District Council as part of its new
three-tier market structure. Music hall and vaudeville artistes of
the first rank like General Tom Thumb and George Robey provided the
lighter side of a range of entertainments that also included concerts
by classical artistes such as the celebrated violinist Kreisler.[1]

The direction and control of this expansion of facilities was the
responsibility of the Local Board of Health and its successor after
1894, the Urban District Council. But their role was an ambivalent
one. Both wanted to promote the interests of the resort by attracting
as many visitors as possible, but despite several attempts to overcome
the statutory prohibitions, were prevented from advertising the town
directly. They also had no authority to provide entertainments and
amusements for visitors, yet, when the need was established but private
enterprise faltered, they stepped in to provide such facilities as the
Victoria Pavilion and Alexandra Theatre in spite of intense opposition
from economy-minded ratepayers. For the most part, however, their
energies were absorbed by the major task of guarding the health and
ensuring the comfort of a population that doubled and sometimes trebled
in the summer months. The improvement of Ilfracombe's public utilities
occupied much of their time; and their responsibilities extended not
only to maintaining the town's water-supply and drainage system, but
also to monitoring the activities of the gas and electricity companies
which had successfully resisted all attempts to municipalise them.[2] On
occasions the local authorities were less than successful - the water
supply dried up in several hot summers, for example, until a costly but
effective new supply from Exmoor was completed in 1904. In other areas
they were more fortunate, notably in purchasing several local beauty
spots threatened by speculative building such as Ropery Meadow in 1872,
Capstone Hill in 1876, Cairn Top and, most imposing of all, Hillsborough
Hill, the town's 'crowning glory' in the 1890s. In 1905, after years of
wrangling, the District Council took over the harbour from the Trustees
of the Lord of the Manor, who had already enlarged and improved it,
adding a pier in the early 1870s and further improvements in 1896, to
enable larger boats to disembark passengers directly without the aid of
small boats. In 1901 96,000 visitors passed through the turnstiles and
the 1911 season figure was almost double this.[3]

1   *Ilfracombe Chronicle*, 31 December 1904, 21 September 1912.

2   See Minutes of Ilfracombe Local Board of Health, and subsequently
     Urban District Council, DRO R2458 A/C 1-25; also PRO MH12/2161-5,
     1893-1900.

3   Select Committee, House of Commons, Ilfracombe Harbour and Improve-
     ment Bill, 1905, DRO RG2458/H18; *Ilfracombe Chronicle*, 18 October
     1913.

The local authority also strove to supervise the physical expansion
of the resort, through its construction bye-laws. The housing stock expanded by almost 40 per cent in the 1880s and by a further 23 per cent
in the 1890s.[1] Residential accommodation especially increased as
Ilfracombe attracted a wealthy retired population. Rows of lodging-
houses also continued to spread higher over the slopes above the town
and into the neighbouring valleys. From the 1880s the town's growing
popularity stimulated a number of larger-scale developments. At its
western end, between the station and the High Street, the Wildercombe
Park Estate was the dream of developer G E Russell for a 'new Ilfracombe'
of detached and semi-detached suburban style villas to let or for sale at
£600-£1500. To the east the Chambercombe Park Estate followed along the
same lines: building began there in the late 1880s and continued into
the 1900s.[2] But much of the new construction took the form of in-filling
between existing developments wherever space permitted, as at Highfield
Road, Cross Park or Greenclose Road. Many of these new properties became
lodging-houses, but from the 1880s an increasing proportion of visitors,
especially large families in search of more economical accommodation than
that provided by the larger hotels, villas or apartments, began staying
at the new private hotels and boarding-houses listed in the proliferating
guide-book literature. Often these were opened by the more successful
lodging-house keepers who had been able to extend their premises along
with their clientele. In the case of the Collingwood Private Hotel on
the front, for instance, the proprietress was able to take over and con-
vert the whole of the former terrace of lodging-houses. More often
entirely new buildings were provided like the imposing Granville
Temperance Boarding House of 1890, boasting the 'Finest Sea and Land
Views' from its cliff-top situation, owned and run by a former lodging-
house keeper, W R Foster, or the Imperial Private Hotel with *en pension*
terms from two guineas per week; and, for those of more modest means,
the Capstone, Rockliffe and numerous other boarding-houses, charging at
the turn of the century about 1s 6d per night, 5s per day or between
one guinea and 36s weekly.[3]

Many of these were built along the new Wilder Road which was completed
in stages between the parish church and the harbour, or on the slopes between it and the High Street. New shops also emerged to supply the increasing number of boarding establishments. In 1884, for example, the
shopping 'Arcade' was opened off High Street, and in the 1890s the first
grocery chain stores made their appearance in Ilfracombe as elsewhere.
Much of old Ilfracombe was also disappearing. A severe fire in July 1896
devastated part of the shopping area, and in the 1890s the Housing of the
Working Classes Act was invoked to demolish a number of insanitary cottages

1   See Table 1.

2   *Ilfracombe Gazette,* 8 November 1884, et seq; *Ilfracombe Chronicle,*
     5 September 1885, 8 September 1888 et seq.

3   *Pearson's gossipy guide to Ilfracombe and the north Devon coast*
     (c.1901) inter alia.

in the harbour area.[1] Gradually many features of the old maritime economy
were submerged in the rush to provide holiday entertainments and accommodation, though the harbour itself remained an indissoluble link with the
past. But the destruction of fishermen's cottages did not lead to their
replacement with more modern working class housing. New development in
the town included little cheap accommodation for the local labour force.

Nevertheless, servicing the rising numbers of visitors, with all its
advantages and disadvantages, had provided an increasingly important outlet for Ilfracombe's indigenous population. In the second half of the
nineteenth century the gradual shift in the town's economic structure,
already underway, became more pronounced, particularly from the mid-1870s,
and by 1914 the functions of the old fishing port had largely been absorbed
by the holiday industry. This process is clearly revealed not only by the
town's physical and municipal growth but by the changing pattern of employment at Ilfracombe from the mid-nineteenth century, when it was included
in the Registrar General's list of eleven coastal resorts and four inland
watering-places to indicate the faster expansion of this kind of town than
of many commercial and manufacturing centres. Between 1871 and 1911 the
absence of adequate census information on occupation, however, makes it
necessary to rely on less reliable directory evidence. Tables 3 and 4,
nevertheless, indicate the main occupational trends at Ilfracombe between
1851 and 1911, on the basis of these sources, though space precludes detailed analysis here of other important social characteristics like
age and sex structure, weighted towards the elderly and female, or the
largely local birth-places of its inhabitants.[2]

By mid-century Ilfracombe was still predominantly a small coastal
service centre with a stagnant population. The port retained something
of its former importance as a source of employment, and the low numbers
engaged in overland transport also confirmed Ilfracombe's dependence on
the sea and its great need to end its isolation by improving its communications. Agriculture was naturally less important within the town, although its close links with its completely rural hinterland were still
relatively strong, and, with the decline of local villages from this time,
many were drawn into the town in search of work. But, with the exception
of domestic servants who formed over a quarter of the female labour force,
the numbers directly engaged in holiday trades remained quite small. Yet
the potential for Ilfracombe's future development as a watering-place can
be seen in the size of the business, trading and construction sectors
from which its resort and residential functions were to develop.

1   *Ilfracombe Gazette*, 3 January 1885; *Ilfracombe Chronicle*, 14 October
     1893 et seq; *Ilfracombe Gazette and Observer*, 1 August 1896.

2   Figures are given both for the occupied population of ten years and
     above, and those of heads of household, at Ilfracombe, for 1851 and
     1871, to enable some comparison to be made with those occupations
     listed later in the 1911 census and the directories. Individual
     entries in the latter are assumed to have been heads of household,
     though, of course, they are inevitably highly selective in their
     occupational coverage, and thus of more limited value.

Table 3

OCCUPATIONS OF THE POPULATION, TEN YEARS AND ABOVE, ILFRACOMBE 1851, 1871 AND 1911

		1851				1871				1911			
		Male		Female		Male		Female		Male		Female	
		No.	%	No.	%	No.	%	No.	%	No.	%	No.	%
1	No occupation	202	24.7	714	53.4	240	20.7	871	48.2	{720	24.4	{2955	63.7
2	Independent means	34	4.2	101	7.6	33	2.8	91	5.0				
3	Professional, white collar	45	5.5	8	0.6	88	7.6	14	0.8	322	10.9	178	3.8
4	Accommodation	24	2.9	41	3.1	42	3.6	138	7.6	305	10.3	295	6.4
5	Shops & crafts	168	20.6	95	7.1	245	21.1	180	10.0	310	10.5	325	7.0
6	Building trades	94	11.5	–	–	224	19.3	–	–	361	12.2	–	–
7	Maritime trades	135	16.5	–	–	101	8.7	2	0.1	{373	12.6	–	–
8	Transport (inland)	13	1.6	–	–	30	2.6	1	0.1			–	–
9	Agriculture	31	3.8	6	0.4	44	3.8	2	0.1	226	7.7	18	0.4
10	Service (domestic)	27	3.3	369	27.6	47	4.0	508	28.1	96	3.2	{824	17.8
11	Labourers (unskilled)	44	5.4	–	–	57	4.9	–	–	102	3.5		
12	Others	–	–	2	0.1	9	0.8	–	–	135	4.6	43	0.9
		817		1336		1160		1807		2950		4638	

Note: 1851 and 1871 figures are for the town only; 1911 for the civil parish

Sources: 1851: PRO HO107/1893; 1871: RG10/21878; 1911: Census of Population

Table 4

OCCUPATIONS OF HEADS OF HOUSEHOLD, ILFRACOMBE 1851-1910 (a)

		1851		1871		1878		1890		1910	
		M	F	M	F	M	F	M	F	M	F
1	No occupation	53	50	58	56	(40	70	(96	114	300	209
2	Independent means	26	47	30	46						
3	Professional etc	30	3	63	3	71	9	122	18	98	9
4	Accommodation	21	25	35	73	109	83	153	98	313	254
5	Shops etc	95	6	136	40	134	33	184	52	212	45
6	Building Trades	57	–	93	– (b)	16	–	47	1	18	1
7	Maritime Trades	67	–	74	1(b)	4	–	16	–	–	–
8	Transport (inland)	9	–	17	1(b)	15	–	24	–	22	–
9	Agriculture	25	–	22	– (a)	40	1	53	2	39	1
10	Service (domestic)	10	20	27	40	–	–	–	–		
11	Labourers	17	1	36	–	–	–	–	–		
12	Others	–	1	5	–	4	1	11	9	10	–
		410	153	596	260	433	197	706	294	1012	519

Notes: a 1851 and 1871 figures are for the town only

       b Heads of household 1851-71 in occupational groups 6-8 include labourers etc not listed in the directories

Sources: 1851: PRO HO107/1893; 1871: RG10/2187; 1878, 1890: W White, *History, gazetteer and directory of Devonshire* (1878, 1890 edns); 1910: *Kelly's Post-Office directory of Devonshire, 1910*

In many ways the gains made between 1851 and 1871 were marginal, and the structural problem of seasonal unemployment was hardly touched. Despite the growth of shops and businesses the role of the primary holiday trades was still far from impressive, employing only 3.6 per cent of occupied males and 7.6 per cent of females. But the decay of the town's traditional occupation structure was becoming more apparent. In some cases old pursuits continued in attenuated form: local boats, for example, often saw service as pleasure craft during the season. But new activities were slow to develop: few more seemed to be engaged in inland transport than earlier although local road services had improved following the opening of the railway to Barnstaple in 1854. With the branch railway to Ilfracombe and harbour improvements under construction, however, the town looked forward by the end of the decade to much more rapid growth that continued throughout the 1880s and early 1890s, and confirmed Ilfracombe's popularity as one of the principal holiday playgrounds of the South West.

During this period the directories indicate the increasing prominence of the holiday industry in the local economy, especially the growing numbers providing accommodation. Before the 1870s lodging-house keeping was still very much a secondary, mainly female occupation, especially attractive to families in which the household head was absent or worked in some form of alternative seasonal employment. By 1911 only Torquay, of Ilfracombe's Devon rivals, employed more female lodging and eating-house keepers. Both also shared in the national decline in domestic servants resulting from the wider opportunities available, especially to women, from the late nineteenth century. But by the 1880s the rising importance of accommodation as a primary source of income is shown by the larger numbers of men involved. Indeed the *Ilfracombe Chronicle* exclaimed: 'One would almost imagine one half of the householders subsist by letting out lodgings' - an obvious exaggeration - nevertheless 30 per cent of directory entries in 1878 and 37 per cent in 1910 were engaged in taking in visitors, though hotel and boarding-house keepers remained a small proportion of these.[1]

In the last quarter of the nineteenth century Ilfracombe also began to increase its residential role for families of independent means - the beginnings of its retirement function. And as its complement of middle class residents and visitors grew, professional and other services like those of shop assistants, building, railway and road transport workers greatly increased, not to mention seasonal casual labour. While its resort and residential functions thus became the key features of Ilfracombe's economy the steady decline in maritime and other traditional employment continued, though the harbour gained a new lease of life as unprecedented numbers of visitors arrived by sea.

Ilfracombe's celebrity in the late Victorian and Edwardian era was not sustained after the Great War. Though the pre-war trend in holiday-

1   *Ilfracombe Chronicle*, 3 July 1880; Census of Population 1911.

making re-emerged in the immediate post-war boom and the resort seemed destined to continue its expansion, the established pattern of holiday-making began to dissolve during the depression years. Arrival lists disappeared from the local papers and in the late 1920s and early 1930s seasonal unemployment became acute. Ilfracombe was among the worst hit of all the major Devon resorts and only gradually, with a redeployment of its accommodation to meet changed holiday and retirement expectations, has it recovered. Despite strenuous attempts to diversify, Ilfracombe today remains substantially as it appeared to Victorian and Edwardian visitors, its physical and socio-economic pattern still largely shaped by their leisure habits. This survey can only provide a glimpse into the changing character and development of the resort they visited and the factors underlying its growth. But their demands and the towns-people's response and initiative still colour the resort, providing an environmental legacy which is now one of the chief attractions for the contemporary visitor.